SCI

APR 2 0 2010

2009
IX 6/10 10/11

Praise for *The Purpose Linked Organization*

"In *The Purpose Linked Organization,* Alaina Love and Marc Cugnon marry purpose and passion into a practical process for growing your business that you do not want to miss!"

—Marshall Goldsmith, bestselling author of
What Got You Here Won't Get You There and the
recently published *Succession: Are You Ready?*

"*The Purpose Linked Organization* explores the most important idea in human capital today. Workers of all ages and generations are realizing what many organizations often miss—we need to feel connected to our work to do it well. Creative and practical, Love and Cugnon offer a framework to help individuals find meaningful work, while offering corporation leaders insights on creating a highly engaged workforce."

—Tamara J. Erickson, author of a trilogy of books
for the generations: *Retire Retirement, Plugged In,*
and *What's Next, Gen X?*

"Love and Cugnon have distinguished themselves as a breakthrough team in the field of leadership development. We've used their tools and processes with great success to develop our emerging leaders. Now everyone has access to their practical wisdom through *The Purpose Linked Organization.* If you're a business leader searching for better ways to develop your organization's talent or an individual longing for more fulfillment at work, don't miss this book!"

—Joseph Pieroni, CEO, Daiichi-Sankyo

"This book provides sound advice for leaders in any organization. Love and Cugnon remind us that passion is a manifestation of inner purpose and offer prescriptions, diagnostic instruments, and wise counsel that will help leaders unlock the purpose and passion in their own organizations."

—Kim Cameron, William Russell Kelly Professor,
Ross School of Business and Professor,
School of Education, University of Michigan

"What are we doing here? Think about how much energy individuals and organizations spend trying to answer—or avoid—that question. This clear and hopeful book gives us a tangible way to capture that most important of intangibles—purpose—and it gives leaders and mentors powerful tools for creating legacies that matter."

—Eric Liu, author of *Guiding Lights:*
How to Mentor—and Find Life's Purpose

"In explaining the role purpose and passion play in our work lives and in giving readers the tools to identify their own passion archetypes, Alaina Love and Marc Cugnon offer both employees and leaders the missing link to boost performance to a level beyond what skills and competence alone will allow."

—Patricia O'Connell, Management Editor, *BusinessWeek*

"Smart leaders instinctively understand that both productivity and innovation would be greatly increased 'if only' they could engage their people fully by putting them in jobs that match their passions and talents; but how? *The Purpose Linked Organization* provides a novel, practical, and no-nonsense approach to help leaders accomplish that goal."

—Henri Lipmanowicz, (former) President of
Merck Intercontinental Region and Japan;
Chairman and Founder of Plexus Institute

"Learning about my passions has made me a better husband, leader, mentor, and department head. I want my whole team to experience this! We can all benefit from understanding our own and our colleagues' archetypes."

—Tim Richardson, Vice President,
Military Services and International Projects,
Boys & Girls Clubs of America

THE

PURPOSE
LINKED
ORGANIZATION

HOW PASSIONATE LEADERS
INSPIRE WINNING TEAMS
AND GREAT RESULTS

ALAINA LOVE
MARC CUGNON

New York   Chicago   San Francisco   Lisbon   London   Madrid   Mexico City
Milan   New Delhi   San Juan   Seoul   Singapore   Sydney   Toronto

The Passion Profiler™, Passion Archetype™, Passion Driven Knowledge Cycle™, and Leading With Purpose™ are trademarks of HRx Renaissance Consortium, Inc., parent company of Purpose Linked Consulting.

1 2 3 4 5 6 7 8 9 0   DOC/DOC   0 1 5 4 3 2 1 0 9

ISBN 978-0-07-162470-1
MHID 0-07-162470-8

McGraw-Hill books are available at special quantity discounts to use as premiums and sales promotions, or for use in corporate training programs. To contact a representative, please visit the Contact Us pages at www.mhprofessional.com.

This book is printed on acid-free paper.

Library of Congress Cataloging-in-Publication Data
Love, Alaina.
  The purpose linked organization : how passionate leaders inspire winning teams and great results / by Alaina Love and Marc Cugnon.—1st ed.
    p. cm.
  Includes bibliographical references.
  ISBN 0-07-162470-8 (alk. paper)
  1. Leadership. 2. Emotions. I. Cugnon, Marc. II. Title.
  HM1261.L68 2009
  658.4'092—dc22

                                                                      2009002444

To Marc, Maude, and Xavier,
may your passions help you to shape a life of meaning

And

To William Edward Reid,
the son of a slave, whose passions and purpose
changed the lives of generations

CONTENTS

FOREWORD

Let me begin by stating that *The Purpose Linked Organization* is a breakthrough in the jungle of "happiness and profitability" books, frameworks, and consultants—a field that spawns more self-proclaimed prophets than actual results. The pragmatic and rigorous framework and tools developed by Love and Cugnon in this book provide leaders and individuals at all levels with a clear pathway to both self-understanding and true organizational performance.

Over the years, I've had the privilege to work with some leaders who exemplify the purpose and passion described herein. One outstanding example is Eleanor Josaitis, the cofounder of Focus: HOPE in inner-city Detroit, which she started with Father William Cunningham in 1968 to provide "intelligent and practical solutions to racism and poverty." Eleanor leads with purpose and passion as she provides food to 45,000 people a month, taking care of impoverished children while their parents are trained as machinists, IT specialists, and manufacturing engineers. She has incredible emotional energy, discipline, and commitment. For her, it is clearly not about pay, not about acclaim, but about passion and purpose. The stories of leaders, like Eleanor, contained within this book, along with Love and Cugnon's process and tools, will help each reader uncover his or her own unique journey.

As a social psychologist trained under Morton Deutsch at Columbia University who, in turn, was a student of Kurt Lewin, the father of modern-day social psychology, I can't resist placing matters in their proper historical context. This book fits within a long tradition in psychology that has focused on the positive, namely the growth elements of individual psychology. These include the works of Abraham Maslow in the 1950s with his hierarchy of needs framework, self-actualization being the highest level of motivational force. Douglas McGregor built upon Maslow's work in the late 1950s with his Theory X and Theory Y managers (the good ones, Theory Y, focus on the development and growth of their colleagues). During the 1950s, the NTL

Institute developed T-Groups and sensitivity training, creating an applied behavioral science academic group with figures such as Warren Bennis, Herb Shepard, Ken Benne, and Edgar Schein at the forefront. In the early 1960s, Rollo May, Carl Rogers, Erich Fromm, and others launched the humanistic psychology movement which later became a division of the American Psychological Association in 1971. The human potential movement started in the 1970s and included all kinds of social experimentation, with Rensis Likert, the University of Michigan founder of the Institute for Social Research, developing his System 4 framework in the late 1960s. This framework was both an organizational and an individual one for full engagement of people by following four tenets: (1) view human resources as an organization's greatest asset; (2) treat every individual with dignity, understanding, support, and warmth; (3) tap the constructive power of groups through visioning and teamwork; and (4) set high performance goals at every level of the organization. The stage for human potential frameworks was set years ago, but it was not until the 1990s that many commercial firms such as Gallup, Towers Perrin, and others began capitalizing on the financial value of selling employee engagement, self-fulfillment, happiness, etc. . . . and thus an industry was born, albeit a troubled one. In a January 2008 article in *The Human Resource Executive*, academic Scott Flander summarized where we currently stand:

> *Despite a burgeoning industry devoted to measuring engagement, there's no established definition of what it actually means . . . there's widespread disagreement over nearly everything else about engagement: whether it's really a new concept, how it should be measured, whether it can be tied to the bottom line . . .*

Love and Cugnon have created a way out of the morass of conflicting claims by consultants and academics operating under the banners of humanistic psychology, human potential, employee engagement, happiness, and emotional intelligence. They provide a very pragmatic and rigorous process for helping individuals and organizations link passion and purpose to organizational performance. This book is a much needed fresh look at combining what leads to high performance for both individuals and organizations. The "positive performance triad" in the book highlights the three key domains that drive individual performance: unique skills, primary passions, and core values. The performance nexus for Love and Cugnon is the overlap of these three domains. Organizations that can create cultures that support this overlap will tap into passion and purpose, thus turbocharging their human capacity. This is a book that helps individuals with their own assessment and planning tools and provides help in charting career paths that tap human spirit, talent, and energy. It's also a solid handbook for both individuals and organizational leaders, as it contains useful diagnostic instruments, pragmatic framing, and action planning guides.

To be a great leader, as Warren Bennis and I wrote in our book *Judgment: How Winning Leaders Make Great Calls*, one has to make sound judgments in three domains: people, strategy, and crisis. *The Purpose Linked Organization* covers all of these areas and provides individuals and organizations with a solid platform for making better people decisions, fitting people to the right roles, and building effective teamwork; making better strategic judgments, that is, where to lead the organization or one's own career strategically; and grounding crises in purpose and passion.

Bottom line: this is not a "let's everyone be happy" book, but a book about how individuals and organizations can be truly high performing.

Noel Tichy, Ph.D.
Bestselling coauthor of *Judgment*
Professor, Management & Organizations
Director, Global Business Partnership
University of Michigan, Ross School of Business

INTRODUCTION

The process of bringing forth the concept of individual purpose as it applies to the world of corporations and bottom-line accountability is one that has evolved for us over the past decade. It is at the core of our personal experiences in the world of business and in our private lives. Through those experiences and our reflections on their meaning and importance in shaping the work environment for millions of employees and leaders across the globe, the substrate was created from which this book was born. But every important transformation begins with a story, so we will both share our personal quests to give ourselves permission to bring all that we are to the work that we do. It is our hope that readers will find between the covers of this book a voice for their own story.

Alaina Love

My journey to understanding how my individual purpose connected with the larger context of the work I was doing began in earnest in 1994, when I was the executive director of human resources for a large pharmaceutical company.

This was a year of great change for the organization. The current CEO, who had been marvelously successful in guiding the company to the kind of incredible results that had made us the darlings of Wall Street, was retiring, and a new executive from outside the company and the industry would be taking his place. Having enjoyed a pleasant, extended relationship with the departing CEO, I was sad to see him leave and wondered what the fate of this high-powered organization and its deep talent pool would be under new leadership. At the same time, I was struggling with a persistent unease about the nature of the work on which I was required to focus.

I was expected to spend time managing the kinds of issues at headquarters in which I had little interest. I had limited time left to attend to the critical actions that supported the bottom line and fulfilled my core—working with the leaders that drove results in the 60 or so countries in which we did business. I found great joy in collaborating with these talented leaders to help them develop their people and their businesses, solve complex organizational challenges, and identify the needed talent to successfully execute strategies. I was less enthusiastic about developing policies and procedures, administering compensation plans, or engaging in other activities associated with the HR function that were less directly connected to driving strategy and achieving results. These functions are clearly important, but they are just not what resonated with my purpose and passions.

As I moved up in the company, my work responsibilities had morphed in a way that took me away from that essential business and people connection that was so vital for me. Hundreds of millions of dollars were at stake, and I was examining the umpteenth revision of a corporate announcement, one that looked disturbingly similar to the first draft that I'd read weeks ago. Despite the fact that business results were for the moment good, I had an uncomfortable feeling that I might be like Nero stroking away at his lyre while Rome burned. But being the dedicated, results-oriented employee I was, I pushed onward in my effort to satisfy the expectations to which I was held accountable.

Having been raised by a strong-willed, driven mother, meeting expectations was not optional; it was central to my existence and self-worth. I am the great-great-granddaughter of a slave, whose son, born just two months after Lincoln abolished slavery, managed to purchase 80 acres of prime farmland in Maryland, build a home for his family, and educate all of his children and grandchildren, despite having no formal education of his own. I come from a stock of individuals who have accomplished the seemingly impossible, making me a poster child for overachievement. The corporate environment of which I was a part was a fertile field for overachievers like me. We routinely nurtured and rewarded stellar performance without acknowledging or addressing the personal costs associated with it. A "no excuse is acceptable, no effort is too great" mentality permeated what was by far the richest assembly of brilliant minds and complex thinkers of which I have ever been a part. Yet I was increasingly forfeiting the essence of who I am to be a member of this elite group.

After one eventful meeting in 1992, I decided that my work life would change, without realizing that my decision would set me off on a 12-year quest to link inner purpose with the roles I play at work. My manager, who was then the vice president of human resources, had called me to his office for my performance review. Sitting there, I should have been thrilled. He acknowledged that by all accounts, my performance and that of my direct reports had been outstanding. We had delivered the desired results for our client groups in a tumultuous business environment, without falling short on even one important objective. He told me I was listed in the succession plan as his replacement upon his retirement. At age 36, I was a coveted high-potential employee and prime corporate property, with an office in the high-rent district of the top floors of a new, lushly designed headquarters building. I traveled extensively, to places that during my childhood I had only expected to visit in books: Rome, Nice, Paris, Amsterdam, Madrid, Singapore, Hong Kong, and an endless list of exotic locales.

And I was, simply put, miserable.

Having said what I thought were all the right things during that meeting, I walked back to my office in a stupor, needing desperately to find a moment alone to sit and reflect. My competent assistant shut my office door and held my calls, while I struggled to get in touch with this new and unfamiliar feeling of disconnection with my oh-so-carefully-planned future. After a few precious moments of peace, I heard the words in my head, "Oh my God, I don't want that job!" I couldn't ignore the fact that the voice was my own.

I was thoroughly shaken. After all, I had spent the last 10 years working to achieve my current level of success. There were no other women in my function at my level and no people of color. I carried with me the hopes and dreams of the generations who had gone before and who would follow me. The responsibility I felt was enormous. The burden, which I carried for another 2 years, nearly cost me myself.

I thought I knew what I wanted to pursue in terms of career goals, but I had failed to factor in how I would carry the essence of who I am to the roles that I was asked to play. Increasingly, my work was taking me away from my core, which, I began to realize on that fateful day, was based on connecting, healing, and transforming organizations and the people who comprised them. This had become intolerable for me.

So, some 22 months later, shovel and pail in hand, I began my long search for a new sandbox. I resigned from the company that had shaped me as a leader and that I had come to identify as an extension of myself. Making the choice to stay or leave was one of the toughest calls of my life. Many of my colleagues, coworkers, friends, and family members were shocked at my decision. I'm sure a few of them questioned my judgment and thought I was making a terrible mistake. In the process, I even lost a few friends and frayed a few relationships. But, despite the reactions of others, I knew I had made the right choice for myself.

In the years that followed, I carried the question about whether my own corporate experience had been unique; like a stone in my shoe, it was a constant, nagging companion. Was I an anomaly, or might there be others like me, desperately waiting for permission to be all that they are in the context of their organizational roles? Were there other leaders who also sensed the importance of bringing the wholeness of who they are to the work environment—their minds, hearts, and inner purpose—certain that better business solutions would result from nonfragmentation of each person's spirit?

It was time to finally take the stone out of my shoe. Contact sheet in hand, I assembled a list of high-potential employees from 14 industries who were willing to share their stories with me. These were talented individuals from Fortune 100 firms, government organizations, hospitals, and nonprofits. They were CEOs, presidents, vice presidents, executive directors, and directors from a diverse representation of work environments. Promising anonymity for them and their organizations, we had rich, intense, and often cathartic discussions about their work and life experiences, during which they shared their joys and sorrows, successes and failures, and fears and challenges, and they described their driving need to engage in work that was connected to their purpose and passions. We'll examine many of their compelling experiences in the following pages. For some, anonymity is still important, and we will respect that. I remain deeply appreciative to all of them for sharing their experiences, whether on the record or off. Their stories and those from other leaders with whom I've spoken with since still resonate with me, as I hope they will with you.

In the months and years that followed these conversations, the formula that would have made my own work experience more fulfilling began to reveal itself. As I talked with these high-potential insiders and worked with leaders through our company, Purpose Linked Consulting, some important themes began to emerge that coalesced into an overarching constant: *Employees are most fulfilled when they do work that is connected to their core driver in life—their purpose.* Organizations benefit significantly when they provide an outlet for employee purpose that connects their employees' passions to the needs of the organization. Passion, I came to understand, is the outward manifestation of deeper inner purpose. As we will see in the upcoming chapters, purpose manifested as passion may be the most powerful untapped lever that organizations have at their disposal to unleash creativity, shape the future, and achieve the kind of positive bottom-line results they never before imagined possible.

Marc Cugnon

Like Alaina, I have spent the lion's share of my career as an executive in the pharmaceutical business progressing through a variety of positions, including my most enjoyable in that industry, where I served as the vice president of the Far East region. I was fortunate to be a part of a business in its heyday, when the brightest minds were assembled to develop and market therapies for some of the most complex diseases humankind has ever encountered. This all-star team of scientists and executives solved tough issues like creating and marketing treatments for high cholesterol, high blood pressure, osteoporosis, asthma, and hepatitis A and B.

We were making a real difference in the treatment of diseases that had high morbidity and mortality rates. My team and I brought scientists and marketers to AIDS-ravaged parts of Thailand to introduce them to children, the most innocent victims of this disease, who were jammed into specialized hospitals/orphanages designed to manage their illness and ease their death. We helped to give a name and a face to the diseases these scientists were working so hard to eradicate. These visits provided a sense of urgency and importance to their work that only looking into the eyes of a dying child can generate. These were the experiences that made my job meaningful and helped me to remember why I had chosen a career in this industry.

Over time, as the leader of the region, I assembled a team of talented executives to help run our business in Asia. I hand selected each person, looking for capable individuals who were able to hit the ground running in this fast-paced business environment—and what an interesting collection of individuals it was! We had a Brit running the business in the Philippines, a Norwegian running the business in China, a French physician leading our business in Singapore, and a New Zealander running Korea, and we had an Israeli as the regional marketing director. Rounding out the group was me, a Belgian, operating in a region that couldn't be more different from my home country or any other region of the world I'd worked in previously. We were a very diverse group that spent the first couple of years learning about one another and figuring out how to work together as a team. Over time, we struggled and made mistakes, but eventually we triumphed, forming one of the most dynamic and productive teams in the company.

However, there is one mistake that has held the greatest meaning for me over the years. It is a mistake that taught me the importance of purpose and passion, a lesson that every leader would do well to remember. It began one November day while I was waiting in our Singapore office for our general manager for Hong Kong to arrive; we'll call him James. He was coming to the meeting at my request, but what he didn't know was that I was planning to fire him.

James had been a brilliant marketing director in the region. He had an incredible ability to develop strategies to address almost any business scenario we might face; and believe me, we were facing many in the unpredictable Far East regulatory environment. While most of us might have struggled with the multitude of directions the business might need to take in order for us to remain at the top of our game, James thrived in the complexity of it all and enjoyed the challenge of solving the Rubik's Cube puzzle of doing business in the region. He was sharp and articulate, and he exuded confidence; and for many years, he performed well beyond my expectations.

The opportunity to reward James for his outstanding contributions came unexpectedly, when the position of general manager for Hong Kong was vacated at a particularly dicey time in the political history of the region. The British were planning to return Hong Kong to China in 1997. Like many multinational companies in Asia at that time, we were carefully planning for alternative business scenarios that might be necessary in order to manage in a new and uncertain political climate. Employees in the region were not without their own worries; they too were unsure of what their world would be like under Chinese rule. Many who had other alternatives chose to leave the region and pursue employment elsewhere. Unfortunately for us, one of those individuals was our general manager (GM), a Hong Kong native, who left the company armed with a Canadian passport.

Left behind were a hundred employees who were uncertain about the future of our organization in the "territory" and who were concerned about their own freedom after 1997. A group that had once been functioning like a well-oiled machine was now slowly grinding along because fear among the employees was increasing as the takeover date neared. I knew that I needed a strong leader in the GM job and needed one fast. James, I thought, would be up to the challenge and would succeed at diffusing the anxiety of our employees so that they could refocus on their work. By this time in my own career, I had made many decisions about appointing capable leaders, but never before had I been so wrong.

James had incredible ability as a strategist, and that's what had impressed me in the past. What I didn't realize until it was too late was that James had more than just ability in this arena; he had a driving passion for conceiving. For him, developing new concepts, strategies, and plans was at the core of what he viewed his purpose to be. I had failed to understand the kind of person James was, beyond his credentials, skills, and track record of success. And my mistake had caused a lot of people a lot of anxiety.

Through James's passion, he perceived that there were very rational answers to address the issue of the takeover. He had developed comprehensive plans to manage any potential outcome from the political shift, and he had clearly articulated his plans to the employees. As a result, he was perplexed with the ongoing emotion in the organization, and he showed little or no sympathy for it. This was, after all, a business issue for which he had answers, so he couldn't understand what everyone was so worried about.

After just a few months in the job, James became a different person—abrasive, cynical, and pessimistic. The employees, despite James's carefully laid out plans, had no confidence in the company's approach to the return of Hong Kong to China. What they needed most at that time was a healer, someone who was able to feel their pain, empathize, and help them to focus on a more positive future. They needed someone to connect with their emotions, but that wasn't happening under their current leadership. I had to face the unpleasant fact that I'd made the wrong decision in appointing James. Morale in the organization was at an all time low and turnover was escalating, so under the circumstances, it was a decision that I had to fix . . . and fix quickly.

It has always been very painful for me to terminate an employee for poor performance, but this time it was particularly difficult. Here was a person who had every reason to succeed and had not. What I realized then, as James's termination package lay face down on my desk, is that he had failed because of me. When that thought slammed into my head, I realized that the outcome of my meeting with James had to change. I had originally hoped that we could agree that a fair termination was best for everyone, but I now realized that firing James would be a poor decision for the organization.

The conversation that I had with James that morning instead turned out to be a very productive discussion. We talked about opportunities for him in a new job designed to explore the marketing possibilities that would emerge from the explosive growth of the Internet and information technology, a job truly resonant with his purpose. James was once again animated, engaged, and passionate, back to the leader who had so impressed me in the past. He accepted the new position with enthusiasm . . . and I think a bit of relief as well.

Not long after this fateful meeting, I appointed a new general manager for Hong Kong, a warm and capable business professional, who happened to be a nurse by training and a passionate healer. Although things turned around with employee morale and productivity, I never forgot the lesson. As a leader, I came to realize that there is much more to employees than their skills and credentials—there's an important X factor that organizations need to harness. My work since then has focused on identifying that factor, so critical to employee success and fulfillment. My commitment is to help other leaders avoid the mistake I made with James, and this book, in part, supports that commitment. For many years after that November morning, I kept his termination package in my desk drawer as a reminder that beyond skills and expertise, purpose and passion make all the difference. My gift to other leaders is *The Purpose Linked Organization*; may it serve as your reminder to look at the whole of each individual and find a home for that whole within the organization.

PART ONE

PURPOSE AND
PASSION

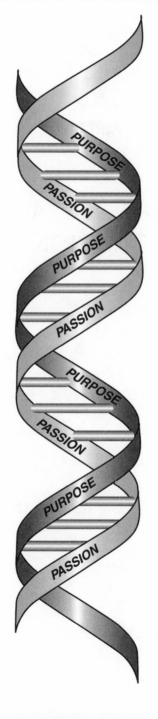

ONE

Why Purpose and Passion Matter

A SMALL BODY OF DETERMINED SPIRITS FIRED BY AN UNQUENCHABLE FAITH IN THEIR MISSION CAN ALTER THE COURSE OF HISTORY.
—MOHANDAS GANDHI

Purpose is such an elusive and esoteric concept that many of us cannot imagine its place in the results-oriented, revenue-driven environments that constitute our daily work world. But purpose, leveraged as carefully as organizations leverage the other strengths available to them, can be a powerful conduit to success.

For us as individuals, purpose is the driver that propels us through life and gives meaning to our daily existence. It's the catapult that can launch us out of bed in the morning with the intent to make a difference during the day ahead. Without purpose, and its outward expression through our passions, life becomes a series of unconnected activities and actions that do not lead to the sense of fulfillment and joy so vital to our well-being.

Consider the average full-time employee. Vacations and holidays aside, most employees spend more than 84,000 hours of their lives at work, a monumental portion of their total waking moments.[1] It's easy to understand how hugely important it might be that these hours at work are spent doing things that are personally meaningful, creative, and imaginative while also enriching the organization and society as a whole.

In the years that we've conducted research on purpose and passion, no one has ever said he or she did not want a life that mattered.

3

Indeed, most of the people we have worked with have been focused on leaving a positive legacy through their work. No one voted in favor of a passionless existence, devoid of the sense of engagement that fervent enthusiasm engenders. Instead, the talented leaders we've spoken to want the time that they spend on their jobs to matter—for more than just a paycheck. Increasingly, we've learned, individuals are searching for a work identity that is an expression of their purpose and passions and a home for that identity *inside* the organization.

It's true that these concepts seem as though they might be more at home in the world of self-help talk shows than in the world of shareholder value. After all, business schools are teaching future leaders about balance sheets and return on assets, not about how to identify and leverage employee purpose and passion . . . it's just too "soft," too imaginary, for the hard-core reality of managing a bottom line.

So why should leaders be concerned about the concepts in this book? Why should they pay as much attention to purpose and passion as they do to market competitors and revenue growth? Because these concepts are anything but soft. Research has proven that while there is a baseline level of pay that individuals expect for their work, offering more money as a means of motivating employees will not lead to greater motivation and commitment to work.[2] In fact, more money may have the reverse impact on motivation and performance, especially if work is devoid of meaning.[3] Purpose and passion are the internal drivers that determine employees' performance and their commitment to the organization, factors that ultimately have a very real impact on business results. Purpose and passion are the mechanisms through which employees find meaning in their work.

These concepts are easier to translate to the work environment than most leaders might think. Purpose, for example, may seem to be merely conceptual—that hard-to-define essence that gives meaning to life. But passion is just the opposite. It's the emotional counterpart to purpose—the fire within, the compass that points people straight to the heart of who they are. Leaders may find it difficult to identify the purpose of each employee, but passion is much easier to discern. While it's the manifestation of something held much deeper in employee consciousness, passion shows up in noticeable ways. It's the sparkle in employees' eyes on a Monday morning; the intensity of their excitement about a new project assignment; the pride that they take in the company's achievements; or the long hours they'll willingly devote to solving a problem, just because it intrigues them. Passion is the visible evidence of our strongest beliefs about the importance of our role in the world. It is the potent emotional substrate that helps us to demonstrate the meaning that our existence and our work hold for us. Passion gives a voice to our purpose.

Psychologists and social scientists have long theorized that the components of a fulfilling and happy life include love, intimacy, and satisfying work.[4] In the years since Freud and others posited this theory, a multitude of skill assessment and career self-efficacy instruments have been developed, most of which measure the degree to which individuals possess a skill or feel self-confident about their ability to perform the tasks associated with their job. In essence, these tools measure what these individuals are likely to be able to do rather than who the individuals are at their core and how who they are contributes to their psychological well-being in a way that impacts their contribution to the organization.

In an era when individuals are seeking roles in which they can "do who they are" rather than "be what they do," it is essential for organizations to identify the specific passions residing in their talent pool and apply those passions to the business of getting results. While employees' skills will always be important to successfully achieve goals, their passions will define the difference between marginal success and flourishing, both for the organization and the individual. Furthermore, research in the field of positive psychology suggests that purpose is a unique predictor of happiness in individualistic societies (such as the United States).[5] In one important study in which one-third of the respondents saw their job as a calling, those respondents worked more hours, missed less work, and reported higher life satisfaction than others doing similar work.[6] This is flourishing in action.

Tightly woven like the strands of the double helix, purpose and passion are life-giving substances. For individuals, they create the vital momentum and sense of possibility that allows them to express all that they are in their work and in their play. For the organization, these substances are equally important components of the company's DNA that contribute to business success. A company with a well-defined purpose and passionate employees who share it can unleash a megawatt boost of employee enthusiasm that can only be born when purpose and passion align. Unfortunately, this is a resource that most companies are not tapping into nearly enough. And, as we'll see in the coming pages, it's a widely available asset that requires nothing more from the organization than an outlet for its expression.

A Search for Fulfillment

Karen Bankston, Ph.D., is the senior vice president and head of the Drake Center, a specialized long-term acute care hospital that is located on the same site with a skilled nursing facility and an assisted living center on a 42-acre campus in Cincinnati, Ohio. Drake is part of Health Alliance, the largest health care system in the area, which owns seven hospitals and has 15,000 employees. Dr. Bankston is among a growing number of talented individuals who have struggled with finding a role in their organizations in which their purpose and passions could flourish.

Having begun her career as a nurse with a hospital in Youngstown, Ohio, Karen spent her early years working as a healer. She enjoyed interacting with patients at the front line of health-care delivery and worked well with other members of the medical staff. Because of her talent for managing people and projects, Karen matured into a capable administrator and later achieved the coveted role of vice president, working for Health Alliance. Along with each change in position came more recognition and more responsibility, as well as the financial independence that the additional compensation resulting from advancement provided for Karen and her family.

But after spending a number of years at this level, Karen became increasingly aware that her accomplishments had come at a price. Working in administration had, over time, disconnected her from what mattered to her most. "I began to realize," she said, "that I had lost touch with what attracted me to medicine in the first place. My purpose, I've discovered, is really about connecting people who need healing to the resources that can make healing happen. And I know that because I'm passionate about it. The role that I was playing in the organization pulled me further and further from my purpose."

At this phase of her career, Karen found herself spending more time managing politics than she wanted to and less time building relationships that impacted patient care. While politics are on the daily menu in the diet of most executives, Karen had gotten her fill of witnessing important decisions being made based on political favoritism. Those decisions, Karen believed, ultimately impacted the quality of patient care that was so central to her purpose. Coupled with this, she felt that management espoused values of integrity, honesty, and respect for everyone, yet they failed to walk the talk themselves. The organization was in turmoil, experiencing great change and facing huge financial challenges, but the team rowing the raft through the white waters of the river wasn't behaving in concert with values that put patients and employees first.

After a period of intense introspection, during which time Karen focused on the toll that her work was taking on her life, she realized that the job was no longer for her. In addition to dealing with the chasm that existed between her current work role and what she felt was important to accomplish, Karen was also trying to manage fallout caused by a boss whose abusive behavior was fracturing the organization. She found herself saddled with healing the organization and helping others to stay afloat emotionally, while at the same time trying to counsel her boss about his behavior. And the more difficult things became financially for the hospital, the more his bad behavior escalated.

The environment had finally become too toxic, and Karen had reached her breaking point. Despite years of hard work delivering results for Health Alliance, she arrived at a pivotal moment in her career when she thought, "I have to get out of here!" Reflecting on it later, Karen realized, "I was getting physically sick, and I began to understand that what was making me sick was my job. The environment in the organization was not allowing me to do what I believed I was there to do. I was running two-thirds of the hospital, and I had gotten big awards for my accomplishments, but I was miserable."

Against the wishes of the head of Health Alliance and numerous colleagues, Karen decided to resign. But so determined was the organization to keep her that it offered her a retention bonus, which Karen promptly refused. Unwilling to take no for an answer, the head of the organization upped the ante financially. However, it didn't have quite the anticipated effect on her decision that senior management intended. Upon receiving the offer, Karen retorted, "It's clear that you don't know me."

The story might have ended here for many other individuals whom we've encountered at just such a career crossroad. Many of the talented leaders we've spoken with point to their role at work as being core to their sense of fulfillment. Living a life of quiet desperation in the wrong job or the wrong organization is not an option that many of them chose. Yes, these are capable people with mortgages to pay and families to feed, like so many of us, but some made courageous decisions to pursue a career that allowed them to express their purpose and passions. Were they frightened? You bet. Were they sure of where to go? Not always. But they inherently knew that staying where they were would not lead to doing work that meant as much to them as it may have meant to the organization. They wanted a life that matters.

Fortunately for Karen, four months after her departure the company asked her to become the chief operating officer (COO) of University Hospital, working for someone that she knew had similar values to her own. The problem boss would no longer be part of her work life, and she thought there was a chance that things had changed. She was happy—for a while.

After a time, the familiar old pattern reemerged, and Karen found herself being promoted to yet another corporate job that once again moved her away from the people who touched the patients. She was dealing with external affairs for the organization; it was a role that despite its importance was less directly connected to patient care. Once again, the organization was in danger of losing her—this time for good. Karen had begun to look for another job outside of the area, and she became a front runner for a job in California.

At about the same time, the Health Alliance organization identified a turnaround project that was perfect for Karen, and it offered her the position that she now holds. Here she has found "the freedom and resources to make the connections that help others heal." In her new job, Karen is able to directly interact with team members who serve patients—from the individuals involved in maintaining a clean facility, to the staff that provides security, to the doctors and nurses who care for the patients. She looks for frequent opportunities to connect with her team, and she enjoys walking the halls of the hospital just to chat with patients and staff and keep her fingers on the pulse of the organization. Karen is where she wants to be—at the front line of patient care, making sure that the hospital delivers the highest-quality service by designing a culture in which everyone's passions can be leveraged.

When we last spoke with Karen, the job was going well and she was exuding the kind of excitement that comes from knowing that you're in exactly the right role and making a positive difference. She has managed to make what was once a financially struggling business into a thriving entity that is running in the black. But along the way, Karen has learned some important lessons about herself as a leader and about her role in life and work. "So much about leadership is about the people," she shared. "Those of us in executive-level jobs can make decisions based only on the information that is filtered to us. The real work is done by those touching the patients—giving the medications, mopping the floors, or making the meals. Otherwise, the hospital is only bricks and mortar. In this new leadership position, I am allowed to be my 'whole me.' I am once again in touch with my purpose and living it every day. If any future role I am asked to play here isn't about that, well, . . . I'm simply not interested."

Seeking a Better Way Forward

Karen's story is all too familiar. Many large organizations undertake the process of defining a corporate mission that serves as the underpinning for their vision of the future. Enormous amounts of time and energy are devoted to developing a few important sentences that can be put to paper, with the intent to create a philosophical framework that catalyzes the organization into action. The mission can be considered the *raison d'être* for the company—that is, the reason for being that is intended to engage employees and propel the business forward. Yet many of these same organizations forfeit the benefits they might otherwise gain from their employees because they fail to connect with the important purpose and passions of those employees.

In this exercise of mission crafting, what large organizations all too often overlook is the direct connection between mission and purpose. We could almost do away with the term "mission statement" and replace it with "purpose statement" for a far more accurate description of what this document is meant to evoke. At its best, a purpose statement engages the hearts and minds of employees and customers alike, pointing the way toward common goals they can collectively embrace. At its worst, the statement becomes a dusty document on the shelves of managers throughout the company—unused, irrelevant, and forgotten. Or worse yet, it becomes the rallying point for employee cynicism when the company fails to live up to the noble ideas the document contains.

What if we could take the concept of purpose statements further by applying it to the single greatest asset of any organization—its people? What if we began to explore and understand what purpose means for the individual rather than merely for the organization? What if businesses could learn to leverage individual purpose and multiply the power of its impact on motivation, creativity, and results in a way that would make a meaningful difference to both employees and organizational results?

Accessing individual purpose would release a new kind of energy for fueling success. We call it "purpose power," and it's the energy that is generated when the finely tuned corporate engine is working at its best. So just imagine the potential purpose power of an organization like Ford Motor Company, which had 300,000 employees worldwide in 2007. Imagine its impact on the generation of ideas, the development of products, the resolution of market challenges, and the quality of service provided to its customers. Imagine the difference that might have made in the destiny of this 105-year-old industry icon. What CEOs wouldn't want an exponential increase in the power of the corporate engine at their fingertips and the ability to harness and apply that power to the business of growing the business?

The remarkable fact is that this kind of energy is easily within the grasp of every business leader, but it is rarely adequately accessed. Too often, the focus of the organization creates an inhospitable culture in which employee potential cannot be fully realized and purpose power becomes stifled. Both the organization and the workers become trapped by the linearity of metrics and processes in which a prescribed input should produce a predictable outcome. These systems, devoid of the connection to individual purpose, forfeit the benefits that would be obtained from unleashing the passions of employees and the creative seeds those passions contain. If organizations could unleash these passions, they would allow a new type of input that would produce refreshingly new outputs—like groundbreaking designs, innovative approaches to the market, and radically transformed customer experiences. Leaders don't need to look externally for the seemingly elusive magic that will grow a company's bottom line. It already exists, internally, within the cadre of talent that comprises the organization.

The New Competitive Edge

Why are so many organizations failing to capitalize on this vital source of success? The reason is that many are simply unaware of the potential that exists in leveraging purpose and passion. Some companies wrestle with these seemingly esoteric concepts and wonder how to make effective use of them for the business, while others believe they are already spending large sums of money on the development of their people and connote dollar amounts with expected results.

While many companies are spending millions of dollars on employee training and development programs, most are doing so without understanding the purpose and passions of the individuals that make the corporate engine hum. Their programs focus on skills or competencies, without delving further into what might provide an outlet for capitalizing on the whole that each individual brings to the business. Most contemporary leadership models on which these programs are based dictate that when skills and competencies are combined with all the right circumstances, the mix should lead to the kind of outstanding leaders the organization is seeking. The concept may seem sound, but reality doesn't support it. Clearly skills and competencies are important, but they address only a part of the whole of each employee. Organizations must remember that even if employees cannot put it into words, their need to express their individual purpose flows as an undercurrent in all that they do. As we saw with Karen, there are certain moments in people's careers when the need for an outlet for that purpose becomes all-consuming. Without it, their journey meanders, their actions lack meaning, and their passion is left unexpressed in their work—a combination likely to leave them disengaged, dispirited, restless, . . . or worse.

At the same time, organizations are feverishly searching for new advantages to compete in the global marketplace. They are seeking the next transformative approach that will help them accelerate the generation of new ideas that will bring unique products to market and shift the size of the court on which the game is played. They want to distinguish themselves from the competition. Yet, as corporate leaders examine ways to become more competitive, what quickly becomes apparent to the seasoned eye is that many organizations have access to similar talent, knowledge, and resources. What truly distinguishes companies from one another is how their talent is maximized so that the organization becomes fueled with imagination—the only true differentiator for success. In freeing the imagination, real distinction might be achieved in the marketplace so that innovative products or services are created that put distance between the organization and its competitors. As Einstein so eloquently pointed out, "Imagination is more important than knowledge. Knowledge is limited. Imagination circles the world."

While the collective corporate skill set will always be an important factor in achieving success, it makes sense for savvy companies to direct dollars to developing a robust talent pool in a way that also capitalizes on the individual purpose and passions of employees. The investment required for achieving the kind of success that can be realized through purpose and passion is actually minimal in the larger context of corporate spending, especially when compared to the negative impact on results experienced when the corporate engine is starved.

What sets purpose and passion apart from other differentiators of success in which the organization might invest is that their effects are both immediate and long lasting. Most management training processes, however well designed, take an extraordinarily long time to bear fruit. But giving employees an opportunity to follow their purpose and passions at work often can and does yield immediate results; it unleashes enthusiasm, dedication, imagination, and creative energy that can be applied to the business next week rather than next year. Unlike other programs, processes, and approaches designed to improve organizational effectiveness, purpose and passion for the individual are abiding constants. They don't need to be maintained or updated; they need only be provided a positive outlet for their expression.

What far too few companies recognize is that their employees' purpose and passions give their companies a sustainable competitive edge. These companies ignore this principle at their peril. Now, more than ever, corporations need the commitment and loyalty of their employees. Faced with a global economic crisis and an aging workforce, companies must maximize their investment in their talent pool so that every dime spent produces at least a dollar in return.

As downsizing and realignment take place within organizations struggling for footing in this troubled marketplace, in the layoff exodus are many of the seasoned employees who hold valuable institutional wisdom and history. Even more of a concern is that many organizations' younger employees are choosing to leave jobs because their psychological requirements for personal fulfillment are changing and are not being met. Where past generations were content to spend their lives with one company, patiently moving up the ladder while deferring personal gratification for their retirement years, today's workers in the younger generations are looking for more—even the baby boomers and even in this market. Money, status, title, and recognition are still important, but they are no longer enough to guarantee that the best and brightest will stay the course. Employees are asking for the organization to shift its focus—to value more than their skills and competencies. The employees want to bring their purpose and passions to work, along with all of their abilities. The business world is now witnessing an unprecedented revolution in the relationship that the individual wants with the corporation.

Throughout this book, we will examine ways that organizations can tap into the powerful energy that employee purpose and passion generates. We'll provide actionable suggestions about how to deploy the resources that are earmarked for employee development so that concepts once thought of as restricted to a learned few can be developed and applied as practical tools that support business success.

Purpose, Passion, and Potential

The journey to purpose and the quest to express passion is a journey cloaked in abundance, possibility, and promise, both for individuals and the organizations of which they are a part—provided that the environment of the organization fosters their growth. In the book *Artful Leadership*, Michael Jones examined the connection between potential and environment: "As we find our own element, we begin to discover our unique and sovereign potential. We come to recognize that our gifts, and the deepest sense of who we may be, are simply seeds of potential. They cannot grow separate from the elements, or soil, that has birthed them."

When organizations offer the right growing medium for employee purpose and passions to flourish, it helps develop a sense of belonging so that employees feel firmly committed to their place within the larger corporate family. This heightened connection is the key to retention of the organizations' top talent, which is particularly critical as organizations struggle in an increasingly competitive global market-place with a labor force that is aging. As our recent research indicates, employees are looking for more fulfillment from the work experience and a deepening tie to their core drivers of personal satisfaction.[7] They want more than just the satisfaction of achieving corporate goals. Employees want an opening that will allow the totality of who they are to be brought to the roles that they play so that the possibility of success at work does not connote a wholesale severing of their own sense of who they are.

When we met with the head of human resources for a large international media organization, she emphasized this very point. She described the company's new plan to focus on defining the employee competencies that will assure its success in the future. This is a company in a challenging industry that has experienced tremendous changes to the way business is done and how customers are served. The company wants to remain a media giant and realizes that to do so will require some improvements in how its talent pool is developed and retained.

The HR head described sharing the new plan with one of the company's high-potential leaders in order to gain feedback and, hopefully, buy-in for the project. Surprisingly, upon review of the plan, the leader asked her, "What's in it for me?" This talented individual saw little benefit to himself or the organization in pursuing success through a focus on just competencies. He saw little connection to the entirety of his abilities, little connection to what he had the potential to bring to the process of delivering results, and little connection to an outlet for his purpose and passions. In short, he saw no expanded avenue for his input to the business, and that's what he was looking for.

Aside from that, the leader had become disillusioned with the spate of development programs that the company had launched in the past, the results of which he felt were less than stellar. These programs had not created more able leaders, nor had they engaged employees enough to assure their extra effort when it was needed and their retention in a competitive talent market. In this leader's opinion, capable people were not being fully utilized, there was insufficient attention being given to their potential, and some were choosing to leave the organization because of it. Given the tremendous strategic challenges the company was facing, this was a loss it couldn't afford. When reflecting on this leader's reaction to the plan, the HR head realized it needed revision. "This program has to be about even more than defining competencies and retaining talent," she shared. "It's got to be about winning the hearts and minds of employees. If we do that, their discretionary effort and commitment to the company will follow." Making that connection improves employees' well-being, which research has demonstrated positively influences performance.[8] Happy workers are also better corporate citizens—they reach out to help others in the organization and develop better social relationships at work.[9]

Introducing purpose and passion into the dialogue and culture of an organization provides an avenue through which a more inclusive concept can take root—a concept that reaches beyond skills and competencies to capture the hearts of employees and put their potential to work. A new creative edge is achieved when organizations realize that employee purpose drives the quality and clarity of employee input to the business. The act of treasuring purpose, and the passions that flow forth from it, permits the products of those passions to create exciting new possibilities for the future. Without the full input of all of its talent, an organization will be capable of delivering on only a small fraction of those possibilities.

TWO

Everyone Has a Passion Profile

ONE DAY I WILL MEET THE LIFE WITHIN ME

THE JOY HIDING INSIDE, MY DAYS PERPLEXED LIKE A PATH IN THE DUST.

I WILL KNOW IT BY GLIMPSES AND FITFUL BREATHS

THAT MAKE MY THOUGHTS FRAGRANT FOR A WHILE . . .

—RABINDRANATH TAGORE

Have you ever wondered what you're really here to accomplish? We don't mean just waking up in the morning and wondering how to start your day or how to wade through the long list of tasks in front of you. But have you ever really wondered what you're here to do that could make a positive difference in your world and in your work? If you have, you're not alone.

Examining our lives for meaning and purpose, searching for something we can feel passionate about, is a fundamental human characteristic. Until now, categorizing that search for a passion has been challenging. Finding a common language to describe it has been even more difficult, especially a language that could be translated for the work environment.

Most of us find that at work, the focus on our personal development is centered on gaining new skills or enhancing the skills we already possess. We may be given certain assignments that are supposed to "stretch" us and expose us to new opportunities to sharpen our skills or strengths or to help us gain a set of experiences that we'll need for future positions. Often we're evaluated at the end of the year and given feedback on how well we've accomplished assigned goals and honed our skills. When our manager provides us with a performance rating, a discussion about our future development may ensue . . . or it may not. What almost never occurs is a focused discussion about our passions.

Think back on your past performance appraisals. When is the last time a manager asked you what you're passionate about or what you believe your purpose to be? Astonishingly, none of the talented individuals we spoke with during our research (all of whom were highly valued by their organizations) were ever asked these questions. Yet all of them could see the benefit of such a discussion in shaping their career choices and deciding on work roles and assignments. A number of them even pointed to mistakes that they'd made in career decisions that could have been avoided simply by understanding their purpose and following their passions. After hearing their stories and learning about their struggles, it seemed to us that there must be a better way for organizations to develop, retain, and apply such vital talent.

In 2005, we began to work in earnest to identify and describe distinct patterns of passion that manifest within organizations and in employees' personal lives. The individuals we met in our client companies were the true catalyst for this study, along with our personal experiences as executives in a multinational company. At all levels in the organizations with which we worked, we encountered an increasing number of individuals asking some of the fundamental questions described earlier. So we committed ourselves to creating a process that could begin to provide some of the answers.

We began by concentrating our study on 80 high-level employees who worked domestically and internationally in a variety of industries, ranging from financial institutions to telecommunications, pharmaceuticals to consulting firms, hospitals to nonprofit agencies, and oil companies to consumer packaged goods firms. As we spoke with leaders in these diverse industries, some interesting patterns of passion began to emerge. After extensive further study and testing with hundreds more leaders, these patterns (which we later labeled "passion archetypes") coalesced into the 10 major passions that will be described in detail in the following chapters.

What's important to note is that the passion archetypes have been further confirmed across a multitude of industries and with over a thousand employees and leaders around the globe. With the new online tool, the Passion Profiler, we are now able to identify and measure these passion archetypes with great reliability and validity. By purchasing this book, you now have access to this powerful tool. Additional details about the Passion Profiler can be found in the FAQ section in the back of the book. That being said, let's now discuss your passions and how understanding them can be helpful in shaping a fulfilling work and life experience.

Discovering Your Passions

Every one of us demonstrates an interest and enthusiasm for certain activities. You may enjoy playing tennis or tending to your flower gardens. Golf might be a favorite pastime, or gourmet cooking could frequently be a weekend pursuit. Maybe you surf, ski, bike, or fish. Some might say they're even "passionate" about these activities. But what we're focusing on in this book is a different quality of passion. It's the form of passion that generates tireless excitement about what we're doing and how it makes a difference in the world—the kind of excitement that keeps us working long into the night, just because we want to. It's passion that is in service to others and extends in impact beyond just ourselves. This is true purpose motivated passion, and it is the birthing ground of the passion archetypes that you carry.

It's true that having the skills, talents, and knowledge for doing a certain job will always be important. After all, skills are indicative of what you can do and can certainly be learned or improved through training and practice. Your talents, however, are an indicator of how you apply those skills—be they inherent skills (like Mozart's gift for music) or skills developed with consistent practice over time (think Tiger Woods and his golf game). Knowledge, on the other hand, is a reflection of what you have learned through a particular course of study or as a result of the wisdom gained through experience. But your passions are the catalyst for all three.

Passion will stimulate you to learn new skills, drive you to apply your inherent talent in creative ways, and cause you to pursue and obtain new knowledge. Passion is what helps the development of skills come more easily to you so that learning is not a chore; it's fun. Passion helps knowledge stick, so you'll remember more about the training program you attended last week than how good the cookies were that were served during the break. Passion is the spark that helps you to be your best and most authentic self.

Some of us are fortunate and discover our passions early on in life. Maybe you fell in love with science in high school and decided on a career as a researcher. Perhaps you were the child who had a special connection to horses and knew for certain that you'd be a large animal veterinarian. For those lucky enough to realize their path early, the choices about schools and areas of study come fairly easily. The career paths to choose from are somewhat obvious. But for many of us, the journey to discovering our passions is a process of trial and error. We move into a course of study in school and get a degree. Perhaps we end up working in a related field, but sometimes we don't. We take on a job or assignment that sounds intriguing at first, only to later discover it's less fulfilling than we thought it would be. As a result, we discover more about what does not strongly appeal to us than we do about what does really engage us. But as inefficient as this process sounds, each new experience helps us to learn a bit more about ourselves and narrow down the large range of places from which we might seek out our passions.

Discovering your true passions can be a complex and sometimes lifelong journey. Because of this, we encourage you to be patient with yourself. Developing a fulfilling work and life experience is rarely an "add water and stir" process. It takes time, a dedication to your own development, and a willingness to explore. It will require receptivity and openness to new ideas; the courage to seek input from others; the tenacity to pursue a deep understanding of yourself; and a sense of certainty that the time you invest in this process will lead to a richer life. We'll discuss more about this journey in Chapter 13, once you've had a chance to discover your Passion Profile and begin to work with it. You'll learn about a framework for accessing purpose and passion that we call "PREP" that will help you to reflect on your Passion Profile and make meaning of it. This framework, along with your commitment to exploring how your passion archetypes manifest in your work and personal life, will provide a platform for creating your best future.

Accessing the Passion Profiler

To discover your Passion Profile, you'll need to utilize the unique access code provided on the reverse side of the back jacket flap of this book and log on to www.thepurposelink.com and click on the Passion Profiler tool.

Following the instructions provided on the Web site, you will progress through a series of questions and answers that will help to reveal your distinct Passion Profile. Since there are no right or wrong answers, this is not a test that you pass or fail. The only requirement for obtaining an accurate result is that you answer the items as honestly as possible. Don't worry about what other people would want you to say and don't labor over every response—just go with your gut.

Your responses to the statements in the Passion Profiler will identify your specific preferences and correlate those with the passion archetypes. The Passion Profiler will then identify your Passion Archetype Cluster, which you'll receive upon completing the tool. It comprises the three archetypes in which you scored highest. This cluster of passions functions collectively to create the "hardwiring" with which you operate at work and in your personal life.

Upon completion of the instrument, you will want to focus on the chapters in this book that relate to the specific archetypes in your cluster so that you can learn more about how those archetypes are being exhibited in your life and in your work. Then you may want to read other chapters that relate to the Passion Archetype Cluster of your colleagues, team members, friends, or family members who have also taken the Passion Profiler in order to discover more about them and how their cluster of passions may interact with your own. If you are a leader of others, it is especially important to understand how the collective passions of your team members interact and contribute to the success of the organization. Making the most of their passions will help you and the team to make the most of the business.

Understanding the Passion Archetype Cluster

The Passion Archetype Cluster defines who you are at your core and provides a roadmap to the environments and situations in which you'll be likely to thrive and find fulfillment. For example, an individual whose Passion Archetype Cluster is Processor/Conceiver/Discoverer may be someone who would thrive and excel in conducting research in aerospace engineering for Boeing but is not likely to be someone who would find fulfillment in marketing the newest fleet of aircraft to Singapore Airlines. Likewise, an individual whose cluster is Builder/Transformer/Connector would wither away if trapped in a laboratory conducting experiment after experiment, with little or no interaction with others and the likelihood that a product of the research was many years away.

The Passion Archetype Cluster is unique to each person and therefore operates differently for each person. Not all individuals with the Builder archetype will operate in the same way in the work environment, anymore than would all 30-year-old females with blue eyes operate the same way. How our Passion Archetype Cluster operates is a function of the degree of relative passion we show for each archetype, the mindset and personal awareness with which we function at work and in our personal lives, and the opportunities we create or have available to us as outlets for those passions.

To understand what a Passion Archetype Cluster might reveal, we'll examine two real cases of individuals who utilized the Passion Profiler and came to understand a good deal more about themselves and their work.

The first example is Louise, a talented executive coach and trainer who works with a variety of high-level leaders in Fortune 500 companies. Louise has a Passion Archetype Cluster of Builder/Transformer/ Healer. The Passion Archetypes Graph in Figure 2.1 was constructed for Louise based on her responses to items in the Passion Profiler. As you can see from the graph, Louise's score for the Builder archetype is at the top of the scale, followed by a high score for Transformer; her Healer score is 11 percent lower. Her results also demonstrate a good deal of Connector passion with some tendency toward the Altruist archetype as well. Louise's results for the other passion archetypes are much less significant.

Over the last six years, Louise has built a very successful training and coaching practice. She's often called in by her clients to work with teams that are undergoing major change, and she is asked to coach the leaders through the process. Louise is a creative individual who has developed some unique tools that assist her in educating her clients about managing large-scale change and redirecting the business to achieve new and desired outcomes. She's also a great negotiator who often helps members of the teams she is working with resolve differences and build alliances.

FIGURE 2. I SAMPLE PASSION ARCHETYPES GRAPH

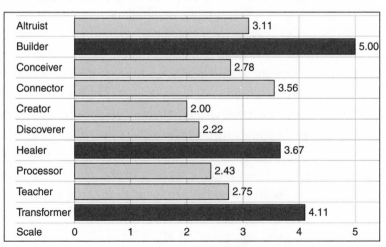

This graph identifies your most prominent Passion Archetypes.

Given the focus of her work, Louise might seem to be utilizing her passion as a Transformer more than any other in her cluster. Yet when we discussed her results, Louise insisted that she saw validity in all three archetypes in her cluster but she felt that the heart of what she does is the result of her Healer passion. In working with organizations experiencing change, Louise easily connects to the pain and fear that employees in such organizations experience, and she understands that their leaders must effectively alleviate those strains on their employees if the changes are to meet the organizations' goals and objectives. Her desire to help organizations heal is the primary passion that motivates Louise. It acts as the platform for the passions that she has for building and transforming organizations, even though her scores for those two archetypes were higher than her Healer score. Louise finds fulfillment in her work when she witnesses how organizations who receive her assistance with transformation are able to create a healthy work environment for their employees, where fear and pain don't overshadow the possibility of a bright future.

Lisa is another example of a leader who has applied what she learned about her passions in a way that has enabled her to lead her organization to achieve outstanding results. Lisa's Passion Archetype Cluster is Altruist/Creator/Teacher. When we met her, she had recently taken a new position as director of development for a nonprofit organization that serves inner city children. A large part of Lisa's responsibilities include developing innovative new fund-raising events and growing the skills of her inexperienced staff so that the organization can increase donated income. Her understanding of her Passion Archetype Cluster is enabling Lisa to leverage her core drivers to achieve the goals of her organization.

The first archetype in her cluster, Altruist, is a perfect fit for Lisa's work in a nonprofit agency that focuses on underprivileged kids. She gains a great sense of personal satisfaction when she's able to raise money to support programs that improve the quality of life for children. And she loves attending the programs to observe firsthand as the kids grow, learn, and have fun.

Lisa's Teacher passion is directly applicable to her efforts to develop and support her staff. When she first came into the job, the staff members were not functioning as a team, partly because they were not professionally trained to do the important work they'd been assigned. For years before her position was created, the members of Lisa's staff functioned like independent contributors, each approaching fund-raising without consistency or a reliable system that worked. Lisa's passion for teaching has helped her mentor and develop a cohesive team. Consequently, the staff members now have the skills, values, and passions to be successful in their work, and they work as a better-coordinated, more productive team than they used to.

Likewise, her Creator archetype is a very valuable passion that Lisa applies when designing new fund-raising programs. As she told us, "There is a difference between being an event planner and planning an event that helps us raise money. For the latter, I have to come up with some pretty unique ideas to make our events stand out among all of the others in this city that compete for donor dollars. I love the challenge. I get really charged up about creating events that spark the emotions of our potential donors, so that by opening their hearts, we also encourage them to open their wallets and contribute."

Lisa's new job is allowing her to leverage all of her passions—and her organization is benefiting significantly, even in these economically challenging times. In the first event that Lisa's group designed (one that they'd conducted for five previous years with no change to revenue results), the organization raised $200,000—a whopping 50 percent increase from the prior year. Clearly, matching passions to roles pays off—in very tangible ways.

Examining your own Passion Archetype Cluster can reveal a lot about how well the work you're doing at present correlates with the passions you carry. As Louise and Lisa discovered, the greater the connection between passion and work, the more fulfilled and successful we can be in our jobs. Understanding our passions can also help us to make better career decisions when navigating through the wide range of choices we may have about jobs, work assignments, or even organizations that we consider joining. If the outlet for our passions is obvious and available, we increase our chance of a good fit, where we can do meaningful work, make a positive contribution to the organization, and create a fulfilling life in the process.

Determining your passions is an important first step in constructing a life of significance and service. Take that step now by completing the Passion Profiler and discover the archetypes that can help you bring the best of who you are to all that you do.

PART TWO

THE PASSION
PROFILES

THREE

The Builder

IF YOU SEEK HIS MONUMENT, LOOK AROUND YOU.
—ANONYMOUS

Profile Overview

No organization could exist without Builders. They are the driving force for growing businesses because they play a critical role in obtaining or expanding a presence in the market. Builders thrive on open landscape and an opportunity to create something new within it. Give them a market to create or dominate and the tools to make it happen, and Builders are in their element.

Builders manifest their passion in a variety of ways. Sometimes it is manifest by a love of physical structure. These are the Builders that envision and create homes, offices, educational campuses, shopping malls, hospitals, and other structures. These Builders are the architects of brick, stone, mortar, and steel who take pleasure in fashioning structural components in a way that complements and supports our existence.

The Builder archetype can also manifest as the architect of the business. These are the individuals within the organization who are passionate about creating new growth opportunities in areas where the company has limited presence or minimal prior experience. They thrive on the challenge associated with transforming an empty landscape into a thriving business environment. For Builders, knowing the objective and the end result the organization would like to achieve is like possessing a compass that helps them create the final blueprint for the business on their own. They are nourished by conversations rich in image, vision, and values and are driven to create business opportunities that reflect them.

Builders are the organizational resources that should be marshaled to create new business possibilities. They are the individuals to send to new countries, territories, or markets where the company would like to establish a robust presence. Given the freedom and resources to do so, Builders will survey the territory, gather what is needed to build the business, and create the revenue and results that make the organization's vision a reality.

Characteristic Strengths

- Drive and entrepreneurial spirit
- Can capably transform vision into reality
- Broad thinkers who easily stay focused on the large scale objectives of a project
- Capacity to work with minimal direction or supervision
- Excellent at overcoming roadblocks to achieving goals
- Generally resilient and resourceful
- Demonstrate an ability to manage external stressors in a way that doesn't impede achieving goals
- Often have engaging personalities, which helps them to attract loyal followers
- Known to infuse the organization with a strong sense of urgency to get results
- Adept developers of others—especially individuals with the same archetype
- Known for "making things happen"

Potential Vulnerabilities

- Can move so quickly that they sometimes leave others behind
- Sometimes impatient and sharp-witted when others do not quickly grasp their vision for the way forward

- May cut corners or limit planning to only that which is minimally necessary in order to hasten progress toward a goal, missing important information or knowledge that might improve outcomes
- Sometimes discount the input of others who are raising valid concerns about potential challenges with a chosen direction
- May not easily delegate to others, especially if others' abilities are unproven
- May focus on results more than the costs required to achieve them
- May not seek input from others as much as is necessary
- Often significantly impatient with bureaucracy

Leading and Managing the Builders

- Builders thrive on goals, missions, and projects in which deliverables are clarified up front.
- They need to be included in creating the direction forward, not just implementing it.
- For Builders, being micromanaged is a source of frustration. Give them space or their passion will be crushed.
- Builders will demand resources, use them up, and then demand more of them. It might be wise to keep an eye on their consumption of resources.
- Builders tend to move faster toward achieving their goals than other archetypes, and they may leave others on the team behind. They might need to be occasionally "reeled in" and course corrected.
- The Builder passion is a particularly strong and lasting driver of behavior. Once individuals have tasted success through this archetype, they won't do well in roles that are not likely to provide the same kind of fulfillment. When they have completed one Builder project, provide them with another to keep them engaged.
- They appreciate constructive criticism—when it consists of practical suggestions.
- They have little tolerance for disingenuousness from those who are assessing their performance.

- They need tangible rewards for their achievements, commensurate with the level of effort they have invested in getting results.
- While Builders resist being micromanaged, they welcome attention and thrive on wide recognition. Managing them is therefore often a hands-on/hands-off dance!

Examples of Roles or Functions in Which This Archetype Thrives

- Country manager, managing director, or business unit head in a new or emerging market
- Vice president, COO, or key leadership position in a start-up business
- Business leader in a rapidly changing market
- Head of a new department, function, or territory that needs to be built
- Real estate development
- Any position that requires broad vision, drive, and passion to execute a mission that completes a once-barren landscape

Supportive Passion Profile Pairings

- **Connector.** Provides support to Builders in identifying where necessary connections can be made to secure support from others, obtain needed resources, and navigate through organizational channels that could potentially delay projects. Connectors are also helpful in developing and maintaining relationships among staff, colleagues, suppliers, customers, and others that Builders may rely on to accomplish goals.
- **Conceiver.** Assists and supports Builders in developing strategic approaches to achieve desired outcomes. Builders will work closely with Conceivers, especially in early phases of a project when establishing a strategic path to a defined vision is essential or when market changes demand a new strategic direction.
- **Processor.** Provides the essential analysis that supports planning for the large projects that Builders may be undertaking. Pro-

cessors are the members of the team that diligently examine the minute details of a procedure, plan, or strategy to be sure that the outcomes intended will be realized.

Special Care Passion Profile Pairings

- **Conceiver.** This archetype can represent both a positive and cautionary pairing with the Builder. In many instances, Conceivers provide invaluable assistance to Builders by helping them analyze issues and directions that might be pursued. Because they are predisposed to analysis and sometimes relentless questioning, on occasion the Conceiver is viewed as a roadblock to progress by the strongly results driven Builder.

- **Processor.** While the Builder can often benefit from the disciplined passion of the Processor archetype, the degree of time and attention that some Processors give to information and data analysis can at times impede the Builder's desire for rapid results. This can cause friction between the two archetypes. Yet, the Processor's appetite for analysis is often beneficial when there is a need for the kind of detailed planning that the Builder would ordinarily move through too quickly.

- **Teacher.** Often fast-paced in their desire to accomplish goals, Builders have in their minds a limited amount of time to review knowledge for the sake of the intellectual exercise alone. As such, they may be at odds with Teachers who want to extensively share their knowledge, which is time-consuming. This situation, coupled with the Builder's sometimes brusque, business-focused manner may leave the Teacher feeling disrespected and unappreciated.

Archetype Examples

Richard Branson.   Founder and CEO of Virgin Atlantic

Bill Gates.   Founder of Microsoft

Thomas Jefferson.   Third U.S. president, founder of the University of Virginia

→ The Builder's Story: Alden J. McDonald, Jr.

Primary profile. *Builder*
Secondary profiles. *Altruist, Connector*

Alden J. McDonald, Jr., is the chief executive of Liberty Bank and Trust, the largest African American–owned bank in New Orleans and arguably one of the most successful banks of its kind in the nation. McDonald, a distinguished-looking man in his sixties, with wavy salt and pepper hair, sparkling brown eyes, and a ready smile, is living the American dream—a dream he built for himself, his family, and his community, despite very humble beginnings.

The son of a waiter and a homemaker, Alden grew up with four siblings in what he describes as a "two-bedroom shack" in the poorest section of New Orleans. "A lot of my skills came from being poor," he said. "They were survival skills. I was poor, so I had to make things happen for myself if I didn't want to stay that way. I've always used obstacles as opportunities, . . . adversity to create new vision."

More than 30 years ago, Alden applied this vision to building a bank that serves low-income customers as well as wealthier clients and large corporate accounts like American Express and Aetna. "I just love to build things, and I look at myself as a change agent," he shared in a recent interview. "Take the bank, for example. We zeroed in on a market that most banks didn't want. Coming from a low-income background, I understood both the needs of the poor and how to make financial institutions work for them. It was building something that was the passion for me. What I did was create [a business] around my personal drivers by developing products to help people like myself grow. I looked at the financial system and thought I knew how to help others navigate through it."

With a strong secondary Passion Profile of the Altruist, Alden made a commitment to change the economic possibilities for the less fortunate in his community. And he took on the challenge of changing a financial system that he feels is broken, the impact of which affects those who can least afford it. "My folks didn't own a house, and I want to make it possible for others to. My father was always late making payments, living from check to check. What I didn't realize at the time is that his creditors were ripping him off so much with finance charges that he'd never get ahead. So it wasn't until my siblings and I bought them one that my parents owned their own home. Because of their experience, I made it my commitment that our bank would have the lowest in fees, recognizing that poor people are good customers too and should be treated fairly. I built my business on this basis."

An energetic and charismatic leader, Alden developed a business model that is founded on converting the needs of the community into economic benefits for the community as well as the company. (It is a model that has been studied and adopted since by other companies in New Orleans.) The leadership team at Liberty Bank made a decision early on that all marketing would be done through community projects. Through working with the community and developing products that were designed to help people, the team believed that they would build loyalty to the bank. And the model is working. As a result, it is mandatory for all officers of the bank to be involved with community boards and projects; their individual performance is evaluated accordingly. The needs of the community are tied to the products, services, goals, and objectives of the bank because Alden believes it makes good business sense. He advises his officers to "figure out how things affect you economically and personally and tie it to your actions." He also encourages his staff to be passionate because he believes passion is the route to success. "I have a passion for everything I do because it relates to me, my family, my community, and my company. I build in to what I do, both personal and business gain. I love to help people, but, as the saying goes, 'You have to do well in order to do good.' It's a phrase we use a lot around here."

Never was Alden's passion for building and skills of survival called upon more than on August 29, 2005, when Hurricane Katrina, one of the most devastating natural disasters in the history of the United States, struck the Gulf Coast. Confident that the bank's hurricane response plan had adequately prepared them for the storm and at the insistence of his daughter, Heidi, and his wife, Rhesa, Alden reluctantly left town with two pairs of shorts, four pairs of underwear, and two pairs of long pants. What he didn't realize at the time is that those would become his sole possessions.

The family traveled to Atlanta and stayed with friends, who along with them watched in horror as the devastation unfolded in New Orleans. The storm hit on a Monday. By Tuesday, it had become apparent that the lives of those from the Big Easy would never be the same. "As the water rose, it dawned on me that the 35 years I'd worked were wiped out overnight," Alden recalled. "I thought, what am I going to do? Where do I start? My life savings are in this business; my home is probably destroyed!"

Not one to waste time mired in self-pity, Alden sprang into action, following a bit of divine intervention. "I pulled myself together and thought about the employees who were depending on us for their jobs," he shared. "I couldn't let myself think of failure because the customers and the employees were relying on us to bounce back. The good Lord told me to get up off my ass and make this thing work!"

Contacting a friend with a bank in Atlanta, Alden obtained permission to set up an office from which he could begin the rebuilding effort. He started by reaching out to Liberty's officers and staff, which in itself was a frustrating experience because the telephone linkage established as part of the bank's hurricane response plan never took into account a complete loss of phone and cellular service. Employees were scattered across the country with no reliable way of communicating with one another.

Once he had contacted the necessary number of employees to get operations restarted, Alden began working on a larger plan to rebuild the bank. He set up operations in Baton Rouge because, at the time, no one was allowed back in New Orleans. Despite that fact, about 10 days later Alden and others found a way to sneak in by boat to get needed files from the office. What they found when they arrived was total destruction. According to Alden, the town looked like an atomic bomb had hit. But the devastation became very personal some 60 days later when he saw his own home for the first time since the storm. "It was totally destroyed," he shared in a voice still shaky from the memory. "Clothes, furniture, anything on the countertops, were thrown all around like a cyclone had come through. Mud residue was all over the house, the porch, the street, and the sidewalks. The bushes in front of my house were even covered with dead fish. We had to walk in with boots, gloves, and air masks to keep from getting sick. Where do you start when you walk into your home and see that everything is gone? I took a few pictures and closed the door. My major focus had to be the bank—there was nothing I could do at home."

After seeing the destruction of his own home, Alden quickly realized that getting employees to return to New Orleans or even to Louisiana would not happen without a plan that included their families. "You must look at employees in a holistic fashion, . . . look at what affects their whole lives," he said. "Our bank had been built on a strong commitment to family, and I look at my employees as family. So when I asked them to come to Baton Rouge and help me rebuild the bank, there was no question that I would support their families as well. For months, we provided breakfast, lunch, and dinner to employees' whole families. After all, where were family members supposed to eat? They had little left, not even a place to make a meal even if they had the food. So the bank provided for them. I was working 16 to 18 hours a day, but the staff had it worse than I did. While I was living with friends and my family was safely in Atlanta, many of them were living 15 people to a house or packed into a hotel room. Some had no clothing, no bedding, and nothing to cook on. We needed to help them deal with [their basic survival needs] so that they could focus on their work. I don't think that my employees would have stuck with me through the rebuilding effort if I didn't value family."

The early days of the rebuilding effort required constant communication with the staff. In order to convince customers that everything would be all right, the staff had to believe it themselves. Their inclusion in the daily business plan progress updates that Alden led helped to keep morale high. "Your staff has to believe you can make it," said Alden. "Not one of ours believed we wouldn't." His holistic focus during the crisis also prompted Alden to tap the family members of employees to work in the bank. He hired them for a variety of jobs, from filing to maintenance. Some had never worked in banking before, yet they even stepped up to the challenge of creating a call center to manage the needs of customers.

The disaster was an event that Alden says tested his ability to build, to be creative, to manage and lead, and to problem solve. All of those skills were needed each day; any shortcomings would quickly become evident. Alden likens the experience after Katrina to "business training on a battlefield where the enemies have sophisticated weapons and you have a bow and arrow." But he is now successfully rebuilding a bank that had eight branches and $350 million in assets prior to the disaster. The road back has not been easy. Little worked well in New Orleans in the days following the storm, and while reconstruction throughout the city has advanced, many, many challenges remain. Despite this, the year after the storm was Liberty Bank's most profitable in history. In fact, based on its return on equity (ROE), Liberty was the twentieth most profitable bank in the nation. And the results for 2007 were even better.

What Alden has called upon in the difficult years that followed Katrina is his passion for building and his model of community. He is working with community leaders, including the mayor, and calling on influential friends and business leaders from around the country to join in the effort to rebuild his beloved city. He has worked with others to set up training programs for all kinds of occupations, from bank tellers to ship welders, turning to those on welfare and offering them an opportunity to contribute to the growth of the city and their own financial wellbeing. In the weeks following a call from the mayor in which Alden was asked for assistance in planning the distribution of federal funds to the needy, Liberty processed $3 million to 100 people, putting a program in place to help the individuals that other banks were turning down.

Alden has seen the results of unleashing passion in his organization, and he is structuring a leadership team for the future. He works diligently to get everyone on the team to buy into the bank's purpose, which he describes as "helping people get to another level in life." Liberty Bank has recruited a group of talented young people whom Alden describes as "fellow Builders." They come to their positions well educated and passionate, with skills that complement what already exists within the team. And like the seasoned Builder that he is, Alden has taken a keen interest in developing these young apprentices.

When asked what he learned from the Katrina experience that could benefit other leaders, and indeed his own team, Alden shared three important observations:

1. *"Planning is a very valuable tool. We had a hurricane plan in place, but not to the extent that we should have. When you look at it, you have to plan for everything in life and plan for a purpose. The storm took me to a whole other level of understanding about what I need to do in life."*

2. *"In times of business challenge, go back to basics and turn obstacles into opportunities. Never say you can't do it. We made loans after Katrina on a 100 percent no-collateral basis. We developed products for the need at the time and our passion was at its basis."*

3. *"What you have today, you may not have tomorrow. But I still have my passion, and it is what has gotten me through."*

In late 2008, we sat down with Alden again to discuss the mortgage lending practices that had substantially contributed to a worldwide economic crisis. We wondered what affect the economic debacle might have on the business model developed by this Builder/Altruist/Connector and how his passions might serve him in yet another challenging situation.

Unlike many of us, Alden was prepared for the downturn in the economy, having identified the toppling house of cards on which subprime lending was built some two and a half years before the crisis became widely evident. Alden serves on the FDIC Committee on Economic Inclusion, and he had raised the issue at a meeting of the task force and had warned colleagues that the subprime market would impact the entire economic system if something wasn't done to correct it.

Despite the potential downturn, Alden remained committed to his business model of lending to the economically challenged, but he instituted additional checks and balances on loan approvals. The bank now looks at customers' skills and their ability to remain employed or to obtain another job. "We're thinking beyond the customers' present status to look at how they'll weather the future," Alden said. "But our business model is sound. We serve a customer base that is always in need, regardless of the economy. Their needs are just different now. We go the extra mile to stretch credit decisions beyond where ordinary banks will go."

The business model is working, and Liberty is surviving the banking crisis better than most competitors. While profit margins for others are down 25 to 50 percent, Liberty has a decrease in profit margin of 15 percent. Delinquency rates were up proportionately to other competitors, and deposit growth was flat in 2008. However, Liberty's earnings were up at year-end.

→ Profile Analysis

The story of Alden McDonald demonstrates the complexity of most of the individuals we encounter in our work and personal lives. While many people may demonstrate a strong primary Passion Profile, the secondary profiles also play a role in how we function in our work and personal endeavors and, indeed, shape the degree of satisfaction we gain from these endeavors. Alden's primary Passion Profile is that of a Builder, as can be seen throughout his life in his desire to create new business and build on existing success. Interestingly, however, it is the Builder archetype that has supported Alden's underlying passion to create better economic opportunities for low-income earners. In short, his Builder passion is supporting his Altruist passion, which, along with his own meager beginnings, was one of the major motivators that initially propelled Alden into a banking career. The interplay between these two profiles is clearly evident in his statement, "You have to do well in order to do good."

We see once again the Builder passion manifest as Alden designs and shapes Liberty Bank's approach to a changed market. Typical of the Builder, he assesses the environment and uses external community needs as a mechanism for directing the kind of product development that leads to strong financial results for the bank. This is an example of a Builder's surveying what appears to others to be a barren business landscape. In doing so, Alden developed a clear vision for how it could be reshaped, and he implemented the strategies that transformed the environment into one of economic abundance for his organization—and his community.

Another key secondary passion that Alden exhibits is that of the Connector. This passion serves the organization well, as it is through the Connector Passion Profile that the inspiration evolves to reach out to the community and develop relationships with its members. While we witness this secondary Passion Profile throughout his story, it was especially evident in the weeks, months, and years that mark Liberty Bank's rebuilding efforts following Hurricane Katrina. Without the Connector archetype, either as a secondary passion held by Alden or present as the primary Passion Profile of someone on his team, it is unlikely that Liberty Bank would have survived the losses that followed the Gulf Coast disaster as well as it has. Indeed, it was the secondary Connector passion that served him so well during the days he sat in that Atlanta office, feverishly contacting bank employees, officers, friends, and colleagues—anyone who might assist with his plan to rebuild the business. Given the ongoing need to restructure the city, Alden continues to be called upon by officials and members of the business community to exercise both his Builder passion and Connector passion. It is the combination of the two that will ultimately benefit Liberty Bank and the future economic viability of New Orleans. It is also serving him currently as he works with the national government and banking leaders to restructure lending to the economically disadvantaged, as the FDIC task force searches for better small loan methods.

Finally, this story reveals an interesting lesson learned by a Builder. Alden conceded a new-found appreciation for the importance of detailed planning, a passion prominent in the Processor archetype.

Detail-oriented Processors can often be a source of frustration to the more impatient Builders whose eyes are fixed on the big picture. Alden McDonald readily admits to having had an epiphany about the value of planning. While it is unlikely that his primary passion will shift far in the direction of a Processor, he has developed a deeper appreciation for the added value that a Passion Profile so different from his own can contribute to the survival—and success—of a business. It will likely inform the teams he builds and the business decisions he makes for years to come.

 FOUR

The Conceiver

THE THIRD-RATE MIND IS ONLY HAPPY WHEN IT IS THINKING
WITH THE MAJORITY. THE SECOND-RATE MIND IS ONLY HAPPY
WHEN IT IS THINKING WITH THE MINORITY. THE FIRST-RATE
MIND IS ONLY HAPPY WHEN IT IS THINKING.
—A. A. MILNE

Profile Overview

Conceivers are the intellectual acrobats of the organization. They are passionate about dissecting concepts, plans, or information in order to develop a greater understanding of the possibilities they present and to apply those possibilities to contemporary challenges. Because of this passion, Conceivers can be counted on to examine issues from multiple angles in order to fully understand their implications in relationship to the larger whole. This archetype comprises big-picture thinkers with broad intellectual interests who gravitate toward uncovering the discrete complexities of a range of issues.

Conceivers are voracious synthesizers of information, which they demonstrate through persistent analysis and questioning. While for some Conceivers, work is most comfortably accomplished alone, for others, analysis is not accomplished in a vacuum. These Conceivers are hungry for discussion with others and seek out opportunities for dialogue because they perceive dialogue to be the foundation of their creative process. The driver for these Conceivers is to uncover new ideas or ways of viewing the situation at hand, which for them is supported by discussion and exploration of issues with peers, colleagues, or friends. Whether social Conceivers or those who prefer to work through ideas on their own, many with this archetype employ a process of query → reflect → challenge as they seek to unravel the complexities of a problem or situation.

Often described as "out-of-the-box" thinkers, Conceivers are likely to be the ones with the "crazy" ideas that others believe would be impossible to accomplish. This is an archetype of courage because their ideas demand strong conviction to successfully implement and achieve. Conceivers add unique value to the organization because they generate new thoughts and abstractions, which in turn feed the creativity of others and fuel the institutional knowledge cycle. In an organization striving to be innovative, Conceivers are a prime asset.

Characteristic Strengths

- Excellent synthesizers of knowledge
- Absorb large volumes of information and identify what is most important
- Passionate strategists
- Develop solutions or see the nuances of a situation long before others are able to do so
- Look well beyond the face value of information, always searching for deeper meaning, and may ask "What else can be learned?" "What are we not seeing that we should?" "Have we thought about doing it this way, rather than that way?"
- Passionate about examining issues from multiple angles; push the organization to examine every possible alternative
- Often the individuals who identify the landmines before others or the organization steps in them
- Help to generate new organizational knowledge

Potential Vulnerabilities

- May overanalyze situations and impede others or themselves from making progress

- Can destabilize conversations by frequently playing the devil's advocate and challenging others on their ideas
- May enjoy the process of conceiving while lacking an interest in overseeing the implementation of their ideas
- Can be seemingly difficult to satisfy and leave others feeling that their hard work is still insufficient to please them
- Can sometimes be perceived as a radical or renegade for resisting conformity
- May dismiss others who do not value ideas as highly as they do
- May be intellectually intimidating to others

Leading and Managing the Conceivers

- Conceivers require an organizational culture that is open to exploration and that values deep thinking.
- They gravitate toward others whom they view as intellectual equals. They work best with leaders who understand and nurture their passion for ideas.
- They pursue all topics that they find intellectually stimulating even if they are not directly relevant to the task at hand.
- Their broad range of interests and their tendency to focus so intensely on a boatload of ideas leaves Conceivers with a huge time management issue. A manager of this archetype will need to help the Conceivers manage multiple interests while not being sidetracked or sidetracking others.
- Conceivers are often not interested in the implementation of their ideas, and they may not be the best individuals for this task. For them, the thrill is centered primarily on the exploration of the idea.
- This is an archetype looking for their leader's thoughtful, evidence-based review of their performance and an appropriate setting and sufficient time to engage in this important discussion—especially if the Conceiver is an organizational renegade. Do not expect to quickly complete a performance review meeting.
- Conceivers may need coaching to help them develop patience with others who do not think as acrobatically as they do.

Examples of Roles or Functions in Which This Archetype Thrives

- Director of strategic planning
- Head of business development
- Director of marketing research and business intelligence
- Marketing strategist
- Research and development scientist
- Long-term planning and sustainability expert
- Futurist
- Business consultant

Supportive Passion Profile Pairings

- **Builder.** Builders will work closely with Conceivers, especially in early phases of a project when establishing a strategic path to a defined vision is essential or when market changes demand a new strategic direction. They are capable of transforming the Conceiver's abstractions into realistic, meaningful, and concrete results.

- **Transformer.** This archetype supports Conceivers in materializing the needed changes that have been identified in the organization. They are the agents of change that Conceivers can count on to translate complex concepts for others.

- **Discoverer.** The Conceivers assist the Discoverers in asking the questions "What if?" and "What do we already know?" They act as the substantial partners in the exploration of ideas and abstract concepts that the Discoverers need to accomplish their goals. The Conceivers often provide the questions; the Discoverers unearth the answers.

- **Creator.** The Creators help the Conceivers to appreciate the unknown and unmanifest. While Conceivers are comfortable with exploring complex ideas and constructs, Creators are masters at developing representations of new ideas and constructs never before imagined so that they can be appreciated by others.

- **Teacher.** As partners to the Conceivers, the Teachers share and assimilate the learning passed on by the Conceivers with others.

In doing so, a Teacher helps to broadly extend the benefit of the Conceiver's intellect.

Special Care Passion Profile Pairings

- **Altruist.** Their tendency to want to address unmet needs quickly may frustrate Conceivers because they are looking for long-term solutions. The Altruist sees needs as an urgency and may view the Conceiver's intellectual processing as an impediment to action.
- **Builder.** This archetype can represent both a supportive and cautionary pairing with the Conceiver. In many instances, the Conceiver provides invaluable assistance to the Builders by helping them to analyze issues and potential directions that might be pursued. Because Conceivers are predisposed to analysis and sometimes relentless questioning, on occasion the strongly results-driven Builders can view them as roadblocks to progress.

Archetype Examples

Alvin Toffler.   Author and futurist
Howard Schultz.   CEO and former chief global strategist of Starbucks
Peter Drucker.   Author and management consultant

 ## The Conceiver's Story: Dr. Peter Lorange

Primary profile. *Conceiver*
Secondary profiles. *Transformer, Teacher*

Peter Lorange has spent more than three decades of his life bringing innovative thinking to universities and business leaders around the globe. For 15 years, he was the president of the International Institute of Management Development (IMD) in Lausanne, Switzerland, arguably one of the top three business schools in the world today. Since retiring as president, Peter remains on the faculty as a professor of strategy, and he also holds the Nestlé Chair. With a distinguished career in higher education, he has served as president of the Norwegian School of Management, and he was on staff at the Wharton School of the University of Pennsylvania and the Sloan School of Management at MIT. He has enjoyed the dream career for a Conceiver: a lifetime spent examining strategic planning, strategic management, and entrepreneurship.

An entrepreneur himself, Peter has built and sold a successful shipping company. He spent years working with companies like Shell, ConocoPhillips, BP, and Exxon, creating a successful platform for international shipping. Through it all, Peter worked across boundaries and through resistance to bring the best ideas forward and apply them to growing the business.

While the study of strategy continues to be seductive to Peter, it was just a starting point in his phenomenal journey. He is keenly interested in applying his passions to revolutionizing the business school education process so that the value proposition of educational institutions will assure their survival in an increasingly complex environment.

Much of the stimulus for the Conceiver in Peter can be traced back to earlier years at Sloan and Wharton. There was a great deal about the aspects of life in a hierarchical university system that he felt restricted the full range of innovative thinking that the business world needs and that universities must offer in order to prosper. In Peter's opinion, business schools must focus their research on practical ways to address the current and emerging marketplace challenges that companies are facing and stay at the cutting edge of what he describes as prescriptive and propositional knowledge. "I was interested in how you could bring new thoughts to the classroom and compare them to standard presumptions in order to create the best learning," he told us. "This led to my focused research on getting thoughts out before they were obsolete. In the standard university environment, most publishing, for example, is obsolete before it's even released!"

The interplay between prescriptive knowledge (based on the learner's experiences) and propositional knowledge (based on faculty research) that Peter described requires a radically different approach to educating future organizational leaders from that being employed by many business schools today. This new approach requires a shift in perspective about the learning relationship, where knowledge is no longer a one-way exchange with the professor/expert delivering his or her knowledge to the novice/learner. It demands that information and learning become a two-way street and available in a real-time manner. This renders the typically long wait between academic manuscript submission and actual publication unsuitable for the speed at which learning must occur in the classroom so that it can be translated in a practical way to the business environment. Without this "learning partnership" between business professors and MBA students (who have practical business experience), the academic value proposition is in jeopardy, from Peter's perspective. "I believe that more team-based research delivers more interesting results," he shared. "The classroom should be international [in composition of students and faculty] to stimulate the best debates."

Making this change a reality required an extensive effort to break down silos in the university, something also common in many organizations that Peter views as a deterrent to progress. To accomplish this, Peter revamped the traditional hierarchical structure, which was similar to the structure found in most institutions of higher education, ultimately replacing it with just three departments. He built a strong team to assist with the transformation, and he credits the team with much of the organization's success. "The very essence of how an organization performs requires working well across functions," he shared. "If you want to be the best in the world, you cannot have silos."

To get ideas flowing and reduce reliance on formal departments at IMD, he has worked aggressively to create "meeting places" within the university. These places can be thought of as receptive environments in which eclectic thinking and a diversity of ideas are welcomed. In fact, it is the foundation around which the institution's programs are built and faculty is recruited. To thrive at IMD, faculty must be self-motivated and enthusiastic about bringing new ideas to the classroom quickly. Those who are interested only in excelling in their own axiomatic silos would likely be unsuccessful.

Peter believes that the IMD learning framework offers an example that might be useful in solving today's economic challenges, where pushing past silos and fostering new ideas can achieve better results. He points to the global banking crisis as one example where "the rather dogmatic views on the economy, the self-regulation proposed by Alan Greenspan, and banks offering subprime lending to create new business was maybe a little too naïve."

Peter believes that there is a more pragmatic need now for co-operation between public and private sectors in banking in order to develop more innovative approaches to resolving the crisis. In a world that is growing flatter and increasingly competitive, not surprisingly, Peter sees more rather than fewer possibilities on the horizon for business. The fascination that Peter has with the flattening of the world is the opportunity that it presents for exploring new ideas and building knowledge. He points to Nestlé S.A. as a good example of a company that is passionate about learning from its customers. "The company is like a [geographic] network of meeting places between consumers and the organization," Peter shared. "The country manager is the constructor of meeting places. He or she is someone who is highly cross-culturally sensitive and is very much a people person." Peter also praises Nestlé's commitment to building relationships in every region and learning from them. Although it's time-consuming and contrary to management thinking in other companies, Peter believes that investments in relationship building will pay off.

What Peter and his team accomplished at IMD is exactly the revolution he desired. Under his aegis, the school has been ranked number 1 in executive education by *Financial Times* and number 1 in MBA education by the *Economist*. "The ultimate objective at IMD is to be the best in the world for both professors and students," he said unpretentiously. "We measure this by financial results. We're very profitable, and we take no government money." IMD also funnels nearly 30 percent of total expenditures back into research in order to stimulate cutting-edge studies that can be translated into course materials and be immediately put to use in the classroom. Amazingly, the university accomplishes these results without hierarchy or titles. "It's important not to overburden an organization with bureaucracy. It crushes passion and innovation," Peter shared.

The magic of the working model at IMD created under Peter's leadership is anchored by the collaborative interaction between faculty and students and between faculty and businesses. This has allowed IMD to produce high quality cross-functional and cross-disciplinary research using companies as the laboratory that informs academic research and underpins it with real-world experience. This ongoing learning collaboration is supplemented by debate in the classroom and through other programs to foster knowledge exchange, such as weekly Webcasts with IMD's learning partners, during which the thousands of executive members around the world can submit their comments and questions. "I was interested in how we could create more effective meeting places where the best ideas could come out," said Peter. "The weekly Webcasts with 23,000 practitioners watching is like *Larry King Live* on the scientific level!"

With such a great track record of success and the intellectual horsepower to think rings around most people, Peter Lorange could be justifiably arrogant and boastful about his accomplishments. Instead, he is refreshingly humble. "Arrogance and impatience are dysfunctional," he told us. "You still have to recognize that you are where you are only because the people want you there and want you to succeed. As a leader, you have to bring the whole team along. It's a 'we-we-we' process. You can't be a 'me-me-me' person and not understand deeply that you are *part* of the organization."

→ Profile Analysis

Peter Lorange is a Conceiver with the nuts-and-bolts aim to succeed and achieve closure on his ambitious concepts. Unlike some with his passion archetype, it is not sufficient to merely develop innovative ideas; Peter's desire has been to put them in action. This is evident in his work at IMD, where he and his team revolutionized business school education and created a highly effective platform for global learning partnerships.

The process for restructuring the school's approach to research and education was one in which Peter applied the approach so typical of Conceivers. He began by asking the question, "How can we create better learning interactions that can make our school the best in the world?" The query so often for Conceivers is the start of a cascade that leads to the further analysis, reflection, and challenge that create outstanding results. The innovations he achieved at IMD are an example of a Conceiver working at his or her best.

Peter faced many challenges while reinventing the school, especially while working to remove layers of hierarchy, which have been hallmarks of a university structure since modern universities were conceived by Alexander von Humboldt in 1804. Demonstrating the renegade behavior common among those with a Conceiver archetype, Peter pushed to turn a 204-year-old idea on its head, and the Transformer in him saw a need to put his concepts into effect immediately. "Why would we continue with the old university system?" Peter said. "You and I wouldn't drive a car that is that old."

As you might imagine, personal interactions have not always been easy for this Conceiver. He has wrestled with pushing others too much, especially professors who didn't want to be pushed into change so quickly. Peter admits to ignoring their resistance and being a bit bombastic about achieving results. So focused was he on the innovation he wanted to implement that he at times left others behind or intimidated them intellectually. Peter insists that his actions were not self-motivated but for the good of the school, although he carries a few scars from the battle and has been hurt when he has felt that he was not understood. Through it all, he has become deeply committed to working across boundaries and within silos in order to remove barriers to new innovations and creativity.

Peter's Teacher passion is evident in his love of learning and desire to share new thinking with others. The "meeting places" he and his team have developed at IMD feed his thirst for knowledge creation as much as they feed the need that he and his fellow Conceivers have for the exchange, debate, and testing of their new ideas. The university in its transformed state has become an incubator for innovative thinking, providing the substrate to fuel Peter's Conceiver passion.

FIVE

The Connector

Profile Overview

Connectors are the bridge builders of the organization. They are passionate about exploring linkages between individuals, between problems and solutions, and between needs and the source of their fulfillment. Connectors make those linkages a reality in both business and personal settings.

In the organization, Connectors are invaluable in alliance building efforts. With their strong ability and desire to see both sides of any issue, Connectors are consensus experts that make the resolution of complex differences more easily achieved. They are often the mediators in dispute situations, able to translate the perspectives of both parties in a way that allows each side to be heard.

Driven by a passion for making connections that will result in the fashioning of an outcome that serves the needs of all, or the higher good, this Passion Profile archetype embraces the concept of "six degrees of separation" and reduces it to less. They are quickly able to see where and how connections might be made, thus reducing the time required to do so. With an inherent ability for network building, Connectors create robust networks of their own, both business and personal, that can be called upon as resources in the bridge building process. While they can be strong independent contributors in a work setting, this archetype understands the value of network building and the power of applying the combined talent of a collective group to address business challenges.

Connectors have an intense curiosity and interest in developing a deep understanding of others' motivations and needs. This makes them particularly adept negotiators who can be counted on to slice through the perceived obstacles to building partnerships. Connectors genuinely like people and welcome the opportunity to interact with others and learn from and about them.

While skills of negotiation and problem resolution can be gained through training, Connectors arrive in the world hardwired with these abilities. For them, negotiating and solving problems are their passion. As such, they have both a trained and intuitive sense for how to create the conditions that will allow a community to be built or a culture to be created in which partnership can thrive.

In their personal lives, Connectors often demonstrate the same passion for creating community that is observed in their behavior in work settings. They are likely to be the individuals orchestrating social events in which a wide variety of interesting personalities are present. Connectors can be observed in action in such settings, navigating through the group to assure that the individuals present have the opportunity to make contacts that will support their interests or their work. They may not segment their social and business contact lists because this archetype does not perceive the need for a boundary between the two.

Characteristic Strengths

- High character judgment abilities
- Intensely interested in how others think and what motivates them
- Passion for many subjects allows the Connector to maneuver across multiple disciplines with ease

- Known to be good listeners and passionate about interacting with others and understanding their points of view and thought processes
- Gifted at developing others by utilizing their network
- Passion for identifying connections between issues and potential solutions to those issues that can be achieved by bringing people together
- Tenaciously pursue truth in an effort to completely understand a situation; able to differentiate between real truth and a reality that others may be creating based on their own biases or hidden agendas
- Usually politically savvy and capable of navigating the organizational arena
- May be frequently sought after by colleagues and upper management for their balanced opinions and thoughtful insights
- Their talent for managing in a challenging political environment is largely supported by an underlying sense of diplomacy and the ability to apply it to most situations that they encounter
- Adept communicators

Potential Vulnerabilities

- May strive for consensus building at the risk of finding the best solution
- In pursuit of honesty, may occasionally bruise the egos of others
- May extend trust in others with whom there is a long-standing relationship beyond the point where trust is warranted
- Often work across hierarchical boundaries with ease, which others can perceive as a threat
- Can become overly burdened with fatigue and distractions caused by frequent unscheduled meetings, phone calls from colleagues or friends seeking help, or external events at which the Connector's presence is desired or essential
- When lacking integrity, can use their passion to derail programs, relationships, or outcomes that others desire

Leading and Managing the Connectors

- Connectors need to see their role as a part of a large context they *fully* understand. To maintain an effective management relationship with them, it is essential to provide full disclosure.
- They often put their own credibility on the line, so truth and trust are important forces in how people with this archetype profile operate.
- Masters at network building, Connectors cover a lot of territory inside and outside the organization, engaging others in the broad vision that has been established. They should not be boxed into narrowly defined roles.
- Connectors usually have an intense fascination with a broad range of topics. They should be matched with broad-minded managers who can create an environment in which the Connectors can flourish.
- Connectors may not be the most disciplined time managers. Attention needs to be paid to timelines and progress toward goals.
- They are comfortable playing a behind-the-scenes role, and it is therefore easy to underestimate the significance of their contribution. However, Connectors are well aware of their own value to the company and will become frustrated if they are too long unrecognized.
- There are situations in which Connectors play such a vital role that little is accomplished without their support and backing. Therefore, their level of influence in the organization can be threatening to others. In the very rare cases where they use their influence unwisely, it can be dangerous—a threat to other employees' stature and credibility among their managers and colleagues.

Examples of Roles or Functions in Which This Archetype Thrives

- Human resources
- Licensing and partnership development

- Representative on new products committee
- Representative on mergers and acquisitions team
- Mediation attorney
- Foreign service diplomat
- Talk show host
- Sales

Supportive Passion Profile Pairings

- **Builder.** Connectors are great assets to Builders, especially with the negotiations or relationship building required to develop a business presence in a new environment.
- **Conceiver.** With a broad interest in many topics, Connectors understand and appreciate the intellectual curiosity of Conceivers and assist in helping them translate their ideas into actionable form.
- **Processor.** Connectors appreciate the information base and structure that Processors provide. They will connect Processors with others who require their expertise.
- **Teacher.** As a prime asset to Teachers, Connectors work to help them identify individuals in the organization that can assist with the development needs of others.

Special Care Passion Profile Pairings

- **All archetypes.** Connectors generally work well with all other passion archetypes. Difficulties in interactions with others are more likely to be due to the Connector's access to levels of hierarchy that others may find threatening and the power base they establish in the organization.

Archetype Examples

Henry Kissinger. Fifty-sixth U.S. Secretary of State, Nobel Peace Prize laureate

Larry King. Television and radio host

→ The Connector's Story: Victor Fung

Primary profile. *Connector*
Secondary profiles. *Builder, Conceiver*

Dr. Victor Fung is the group chairman of 102-year-old Li & Fung group of companies, a Hong Kong–based global outsourcing and supply chain management firm that operates in 40 countries, employs 11,000 people, and generates over $12 billion in annual revenue. He is the grandson of the company's founder, who started the firm with a partner in the early 1900s in Canton (Guangzhou), China. Originally, the company focused primarily on exports of porcelain, antiques, and silk. U.S.-educated Victor, along with his brother, William, have revolutionized this once privately owned company and made it a force to be reckoned with in the global distribution business arena.

The process of building Li & Fung to its current envious stature has been an effort undertaken over the last 25 years by the two brothers working collaboratively. When they both returned from graduate school at Harvard (Victor with a Ph.D. in business economics and William with an MBA), much of what they had learned about growing a business was not applicable in Asia at the time. Instead of being able to utilize contemporary techniques for growing a business, the brothers found themselves in an environment where relationships reigned supreme. If a business was to be built, its success would depend upon the relationships its leaders developed in the region. For Victor, the consummate Connector, it was a challenge for which he was uniquely well suited.

Brilliant, energetic, and intellectually curious, Victor epitomizes the vibrancy of Hong Kong. His ease in any culture, excellent character judgment, good listening skills, and boundless enthusiasm about business possibilities allowed Victor to develop the much-needed relationships in the early years of heading Li & Fung. But as the company grew, the brothers discovered that it wasn't possible to continue to operate solely based on relationships. "Large numbers of people were making decisions every day," Victor reflected, "so we needed a structure and certain systems in order to function effectively. Suddenly everything we had learned in business school became relevant." The brothers implemented dramatic changes in the way the company was structured, and Victor's passion for connecting remained a distinct advantage throughout the transition.

Under his leadership, the company developed an operating framework that was Asian in its values but Western in its architecture. Li & Fung was a family company, with the long-term steadiness of vision that provides, but with Victor at the helm it functioned as a meritocracy. He took a lead role in setting the strategic direction of the organization, and instead of creating the five-year rolling plans found in many Western companies, he advocated a fixed three-year planning cycle. In Victor's opinion, this way of operating provides managers with a period of stability in which to perform, but it also requires that he remain in frequent communication with the staff in order to stay the course. "I feel that it's very important to communicate the strategic direction *constantly*," he shared. "I must be very, very stable in my message in order to be the compass or the lighthouse for the organization.

With his strong Connector passion, Victor thrives in this role. He conducts frequent conferences and town hall meetings to reach out to employees around the world. In addition, he devotes a lot of face time to customers and business unit heads and spends roughly 180 days a year on the road. He's a proponent of open access to leadership and believes it's important to be approachable and a good listener. "Even though you have power over people, you must win their trust," Victor shared. "As a leader, you may be able to dictate, but that doesn't matter because unless you can motivate the guy at the bottom of the rung, you can't win."

Victor's Connector passion became a valuable asset when the company needed to address the fragmentation of its logistics function and centralize 150 different business units. "I personally conducted a series of meetings to bring folks together to gather ideas," he remembered. "We then set up beta sites [to test out those ideas] and brought people to experience those sites. We let them ask questions and get used to this new way of doing things. Then, we continued to test further. And we did all of this before implementing [the new structure] broadly. Now people wonder why we ever did things any other way." It was Victor's passion to reach employees at all levels that made the project transition so successfully. With the centralization of logistics, the company now has a competitive advantage that has resulted in a reduction of $75 million per year in operating costs.

The Connector in Victor has also allowed the organization to leverage knowledge in a way that achieves results. The trading business alone consists of 15,000 people, whom Victor believes collectively have the most expertise in the world in the consumer durable goods business. With all of this knowledge residing in the heads of people located in 40 different countries, relationship building has become the mechanism through which Victor achieves knowledge sharing. "When leaders are talking with customers, I have to be sure that they're not talking as strangers, but as friends. Even when we have conferences [to which customers are invited], I tell my people that half of the objective is social."

The company carries Victor's passion for connecting even to the design of its offices. Informal meeting spaces are planned into the architecture because, according to this leader, "the best ideas and solutions come when sharing a cup of coffee." It is this drive to connect with others that is the hallmark of Victor's leadership. "I haven't found a better way to discover someone's passions than to spend time with the individual working person to person," he said. "Then I have a real sense of who that person is."

He effectively applied this philosophy in the process of expanding the Li & Fung empire, as he acquired other companies to add to the portfolio. Victor implemented a standing rule that no deal would be closed until he had personally visited the company owners to observe them in their own work environment. "Spending an hour or two [with the company's leaders] in their natural habitat gives me a huge amount of information about them," he insists.

Like many Connectors, Victor genuinely enjoys people. He's a high-energy person, conversant on many topics, and his interactions with others are more than a means to a business end. In conversation with him, you have the sense that he is fully present; his eyes don't roam the room searching for a more important person with whom to speak. "I never think that I am wasting my time while talking with someone," said Victor. "I think there is something you can learn from everyone. So when I attend parties, I grab a drink and charge into the biggest crowd I can find!"

➔ Profile Analysis

Without Victor Fung's ability to reach out to and engage employees at all levels, the mammoth undertaking to centralize Li & Fung's distribution system might have turned out quite differently and the company might not be enjoying its reputation as a global outsourcing leader. No doubt his deep skill training in business economics was a factor in the company's success, but this passionate Connector also understood the importance of the human element in growing the century-old business. He utilized his intense interest in people to build a multibillion-dollar conglomerate, perhaps well beyond the expectations of the company's founders.

Typical of Connectors, Victor worked all levels of the organization in order to share his vision and ensure that the way forward was clearly understood by everyone. Like others of his archetype, he makes himself broadly accessible so that he can keep his finger on the pulse of the organization and the regions in which it operates. To do so, he maintains a fluid interaction between business and personal contacts. It is not unusual to receive a call from Victor in the morning with a request to "get together for a quiet lunch" that same afternoon and find yourself in a restaurant with 20 of his friends and business associates—the Connector always looking for opportunities to bring people together to share ideas. His extensive travel schedules, intense interests in a broad range of subjects, and memberships in over 50 clubs and organizations just provide more opportunities for his passion to flourish.

Victor's Conceiver passion played a big role in how Li & Fung developed and grew its capabilities. He recognized the value of strategic acquisitions, and he identified the most advantageous companies for Li & Fung to acquire. With his strong Builder passion, he spent a good deal of the early years of the growth process traveling and putting deals together, so that Li & Fung could achieve its strategic vision to be a global supply chain management company. He also recognized the power of the institutional wisdom the company was developing, and he relied on his Connector passion to create opportunities to share and spread knowledge, with the firm belief that relationships, rather than knowledge management systems, were the best ways to accomplish this goal.

As a leader, Victor has not lost sight of the fact that results are accomplished through people. He understands that employee loyalty and trust are precious commodities and works hard to retain them. When Li & Fung celebrated its hundred-year anniversary in 2006, rather than implementing a broad external publicity campaign, he decided the celebration should be an internal affair. In recognition of the employee base that had made the company's success possible, Li & Fung rented Disneyland in Hong Kong for the day and invited employees and their families to enjoy the festivities. In Victor's opinion, relationships are built on trust and loyalty that must extend beyond the employees to their families as well. From Victor's perspective, the collateral benefit of the goodwill generated by the company's celebration in Disneyland far exceeded what could have resulted from any external publicity campaign the company might have launched.

SIX

The Creator

EVERYTHING VANISHES AROUND ME, AND WORKS ARE BORN AS IF
OUT OF THE VOID. RIPE, GRAPHIC FRUITS FALL OFF. MY HAND HAS
BECOME THE OBEDIENT INSTRUMENT OF A REMOTE WILL.
—PAUL KLEE

Profile Overview

Creators are the artisans of the organization. Their thought patterns are anything but linear; instead they are filled with images, emotions, and elements that appeal to the senses. They are artists in a variety of fields such as marketing, software design, merchandise design, fashion design, photography, culinary arts, landscape design, music, theater, writing, painting, or other traditional artistic endeavors.

The language of the Creators is rich in possibilities and indeed without limitations. They thrive on challenges and unaddressed needs, and they eagerly imagine potential solutions or representations that they could design into being. These are designs that spring forth from the active imagination of the Creators, and they cannot be controlled into existence. Neither can the internal processes that birth the designs and ideas be turned on or off by the Creators.

The idea drives the actions of the Creator. And in some cases, the drive is implacable, leaving the Creator exhausted from the idea's unrelenting mental pestering. The idea does not rest, nor does the Creator, until a form of it has been developed. This archetype, then, is the ripe vessel from which true art emerges.

While Creators are comfortable with the intellectual exploration of a challenging problem, an unmet need, or an unexplored idea, intellectual exploration alone does not provide the fulfillment they seek. As Creators hold a concept in mind, their passion drives them to birth their ideas through artistic expression. Most Creators find it difficult to rest until their pursuit of an ideal external expression of what they hold as an internal mental construct has been successfully achieved. For this archetype, the joy is in creating a reality for others from the reality they hold in their own consciousness.

Creators often examine challenges or perceive an unaddressed need and easily imagine potential solutions. Whether it is a hot new video game, an award-winning advertisement, a Broadway play, or a symphony, the work of the Creators is to translate concepts into tangible models that can be shared with or experienced by others. The model may take on many forms: the written word, music, an image, or a structure. The *type* of form is determined by the innate skills of the Creators; however, the *drive to produce* the form is the heart of this archetype. Ultimately, the passion of the Creators is to pay homage to the beauty they perceive and manifest the extraordinary.

It is important to note that not all Creators develop artistic representations that are designed to be solutions to a challenge. Instead, they may develop an imaginative representation of the challenge itself, rather than the tangible form of a solution. Consider, for example, the multitude of films, books, and songs about the same themes: lost love, overcoming a burden, triumph of the underdog, the adventure story, and so on. These themes represent the Creator's manifestation of the challenge, not necessarily resolution of it (as not every story has a happy ending). So there are some individuals of this archetype whose passion drives them to develop manifestations of a challenge or issue, while others of this archetype are driven to develop tangible representations of a solution to the problem. Both Creator types add value. Those who develop tangible solutions provide creative new products from which others may benefit, while those who develop representations of the challenge provide a mechanism through which it might be better understood and ultimately resolved.

Because of their deep connection to that which touches the emotion, many Creators are able to inspire others. They internalize that which they observe or imagine and find a way to translate it through their own emotional filters to produce an outcome that others can feel. This ability results in the joy, sorrow, awe, or peace that others may feel when experiencing the work of this archetype.

Creators possess incredible imaginations. Their thought patterns lead to what-if questions that allow them to design representations that others may never have conceived. This is the archetype that has allowed organizations to leap forward, as they carry others along with them to new worlds accessed only through imagination. The Creator's what-if questions have produced outcomes of both immense beauty and amazing functionality: the Sistine Chapel; the Taj Majal; the ability to survive a terminal disease because of the creation of artificial organs; a credit card–sized tool that stores 20,000 songs for our listening enjoyment; and the ability to compete in a football game merely by holding a joystick. While some of these products are the work of the Creators alone, others may be the joint effort of Creators working with other archetypes such as Conceivers and Builders. What is certain is that the Creators see endless potential for manifesting beauty and originality when the starting point is the imagination.

Characteristic Strengths

- Incredible imagination
- Strong creative energy and enthusiasm
- Deep and abiding connection to emotion
- Ability to inspire others through their work
- Strong determination to correctly manifest that which they hold as a mental construct
- High degree of openness to possibility
- Appreciation for beauty or functionality
- Compelled to create what doesn't yet exist

Potential Vulnerabilities

- May be overly sensitive to criticism about their work because their work is an integral part of themselves
- May be absorbed with their work to the exclusion of other important issues
- May be disorganized
- May be somewhat resistant to rules
- May be insensitive to time constraints
- May find it difficult to disconnect from emotion at times when logic is required
- May be overly driven to develop an ideal for what they hold in their imagination
- May be driven to represent a challenge in physical form but not driven to actually resolve it

Leading and Managing the Creators

- Creators' fertile imaginations take them to unexpected places. This is an archetype that requires freedom. With Creators, be prepared to expect the unexpected.
- They need to find a mental space in which to work. When in this "zone," Creators might at times be hard to reach. If not invited in, it is best to leave Creators alone so as not to disturb their work process.
- Creators are often extremely sensitive. Leaders of this archetype should be very tactful when providing direction or criticism.
- Creators are by nature unconcerned with timelines or deadlines; therefore, prudent managers must factor this reality into work plans.
- Creators are an unstoppable source of ideas—good or bad, applicable or not. It is the role of the manager of this archetype to channel their creative energy appropriately.

Examples of Roles or Functions in Which This Archetype Thrives

- Writer
- Visual and dramatic arts
- Musician and/or composer
- Advertising and promotion
- Merchandise and fashion design
- Graphic artist
- Software design
- Chef
- Landscape architect
- Film maker
- Photographic journalist

Supportive Passion Profile Pairings

- **Conceiver.** A fellow archetype of ideas and concepts, a Conceiver will work well with a Creator in developing innovations. The Creator will help the ideas of both archetypes be manifest in a form that can be shared with others.
- **Builder.** Creators assist Builders by translating the Builders' vision, held as a mental construct, into a variety of forms that others might understand more fully and connect with emotionally.

Special Care Passion Profile Pairings

- **Processor.** As an archetype that operates best in limited structure, the Creators may resist the structure that the Processors wish to establish and push against the Processors' practical tendencies.

Archetype Examples

Leonardo da Vinci. Renaissance painter, sculptor, inventor
Steven Spielberg. Film maker
Kahlil Gibran. Poet, painter
Coco Chanel. Fashion designer
Ansel Adams. Photographer

The Creator's Story: Chris Johns

Primary profile. *Creator*
Secondary profiles. *Discoverer, Altruist*

Like many young people from families of modest means who live in small rural towns, Chris Johns got his first taste of the exotic places the world has to offer through the pages of the *National Geographic* magazine. He spent hours perusing old issues of its iconic yellow-bordered covers when visiting his grandparents, who had an ample collection of the publication. "The pictures in the magazines made me want to visit those places," he remembered. "It is what nurtured the wanderlust in me."

Little did he know at the time what the future would hold. Chris Johns, the young boy curled up on his grandparents' sofa, traveling the world through pictures in old magazines, went on to become one of the most gifted wildlife photographers on the planet and the editor in chief of *National Geographic* magazine. He has since won a spate of awards for his own work, and he has transformed the magazine to such an extent that it has won every major magazine award over the last three years.

While a student at Oregon State, Chris thought he'd pursue his love of animals by studying to become a veterinarian, but he quickly discovered that his passion for literature and journalism far exceeded his abilities in science. When his roommate brought a camera back to the dorm one day, it marked the seminal moment that launched a lifelong journey of capturing the world in pictures. While on a visit to the school in his junior year, his father asked Chris what he wanted to become. By then Chris had determined that he wanted a career in photojournalism, so he shared this news with his father. His father (whom Chris described as a man of great intellectual ability) chose only five words in reply to his son's declaration: "Just be a good one," he told him. Those words became an unrestricted ticket for Chris to explore and develop his art.

Over the following years, Chris pursued his passion, working first as a newspaper journalist, learning how to be a good photographer as well as a good writer. While studying under R. Smith Schuneman in graduate school at the University of Minnesota, Chris learned that his love of photography brought along with it a responsibility to the body of work within his field. "This is your craft, your profession," Schuneman told him. "What will you do to advance it?"

Chris has shouldered this responsibility well throughout his career by maintaining high quality standards for his own work and for that of others at the magazine. Over time, because of his commitment to his work, he has subjected himself to some pretty tough criticism. The most memorable feedback came during his first assignment in Japan for *National Geographic* magazine. Having never visited the "Land of the Rising Sun," Chris found himself overwhelmed by the magic of the country. While photographing a ceremonial event on location, he became even more awestruck by the costumes and the pageantry. Chris snapped photo after photo that day, sure that he'd gotten some fabulous shots. Was it possible that one was even good enough for the cover of the magazine?

Since those were the days before digital photography and immediate gratification, Chris shipped rolls of pictures back to his photo editor, Susan Welchman, and waited impatiently for them to be developed. When he spoke to her later about his work, sure that she would share his excitement, Susan delivered her verdict: "You quit too soon! You became infatuated with the outfits. People who have traveled all over the world and have seen all kinds of things read this magazine. You haven't shown them anything new."

That was tough criticism for Chris—Creators take feedback quite personally because their work is such an extension of themselves. Deflated but determined, Chris looked at the best work in the world and decided, "I want to be that good. Therefore, I'll go out of my way to seek help to refine my vision."

So he became a sponge—working to clarify his aesthetic sense. "In the beginning of your career, you'll imitate what you see," Chris explained. "Over time you'll develop your own style." At some point

Chris began to ask himself, "What stories can *I* tell? What images can *I* make?" His willingness to explore these important questions has allowed him to tell stories through his photographs in a way that no one else has ever told them.

On one memorable photo expedition in Africa, Chris and his crew were shooting a story on a herd of cheetah that the team had been tracking for five weeks. Cheetahs are an endangered species that Chris felt privileged to be able to film. He wanted to understand this animal—to learn how it lived, learn how it thought, and learn how it survived. For weeks he watched young cubs play and frolic, imitate the stalking behavior of hunting adults, run at fantastic speeds and leap into the air—as only a cheetah can do. Chris became particularly attached to the herd, and he worked tirelessly to document their beauty, hoping it would show the world why protecting their survival is so essential. This became the motive for his pictures and the impetus for capturing just the right shot. "When you're there with your camera, you have to be *in the moment*," he emphatically stated. "You can't be thinking about anything else. You must be completely committed and fueled by passion. You have to know, this is where you're supposed to be *right now*. It's a zone, . . . and you really learn to cherish the zones."

That zone brought Chris to one of the most profound moments of his life during the expedition. While crouching next to his Land Rover, behind nothing more than a long lens and a tripod, Chris watched as one cheetah broke away from the pack and headed in his direction. This graceful, swift, and dangerous animal began sniffing and nibbling on the camera lens—a mere three feet away from Chris. Sitting quietly, not daring to move, Chris's hand rested lightly on the tripod. The cheetah inched closer, wary eyes carefully gauging this stranger. She moved closer still and sniffed his hand, then gently began licking his fingers. Chris had been accepted. This wild animal felt safe with him. She lay down near the camera for just a moment before quietly strolling back to the herd; Chris, meanwhile, found himself in tears.

Typical of a Creator, Chris wants those who view his photographs to experience the emotion of the moment he has captured. He's constantly in search of the very best shot, working his subject from all possible angles, chasing the light until the perfect moment presents itself to the lens, . . . and then never being quite satisfied that he has gotten it exactly right. He's brutally demanding of himself, this Creator, and at the same time profusely complimentary of those whose work he admires.

His decision to move into management at the magazine was in part fueled by his pursuit of perfection in his own work and the toll it takes on other parts of his life. "I made the decision to discontinue being a field photographer because I can't be the husband and father that I want to be," he candidly shared. "The longer I did it, the more frightened I became that I couldn't do the work up to my standards. I kept raising the bar. I was gone all the time, . . . thinking about the work all the time. There wasn't much room for anything else." Surprisingly, with a prodigious portfolio of work that others would feel proud to claim as their own, Chris Johns has not one of his own pictures hanging on the walls of his home. When he looks at them, he sees all the flaws.

Chris admits that there is depth to the patina of his work as he has grown older, but at the same time, he retains a drive that makes him want to continue to improve. "As a photographer, there are rich experiences that you have," he told us. "You tend to find your camera and think to yourself, 'Show me what you see, . . . show me what you feel.' Invariably though, you fall short. You can never quite capture what you felt. That mental pestering about getting the best shot doesn't leave you alone, but it does get you up in the morning."

Chris has now moved on in his career from photographer to editor in chief, which presents a new set of opportunities and complexities. He's a Creator who must lead and motivate other Creators, while still holding them accountable to the high standards that the magazine has established and that readers expect. He's leading through challenging times in an environment where consumer expectations are that information should be free. These competitive challenges have led other publications to scale back and seek low-cost alternatives to delivering information, some of which may compromise quality. But Chris remains resolute that the standards of journalism at the *National Geo-*

graphic will remain high. "What we want to do is provide people with information and experiences on the pages of the magazine and on the Web that help them to make good decisions," he shared. "I want our readers to be able to say that *National Geographic* magazine was saying things that really needed to be said."

When we asked him to reflect on his life and work and what he aspires to contribute to his art, Chris focused instead on the impact that he hopes his work, and the magazine, will have on the world. "The earth is changing so quickly," he reflected, "that it's our job to document it and show it to future generations. At *National Geographic* magazine, the power of photography helps us to see with clarity what's truly important. The way we do this is to send people out to be a witness to what's going on in the world and come back with a voice—one that's nonjudgmental, but passionate. I do think a lot about what I want people to say about me when I'm gone. I hope that they'll say, 'He made a difference.'"

→ Profile Analysis

The Creator's passion is a fire that once kindled, rarely goes out. We see in Chris Johns a spark that started early in life, with his love of photography, animals, and travel, that blossomed into a career of substantive achievement. His work as a photographer is the mechanism through which the Creator in him seeks to touch the emotions of others by capturing the splendor of the world around us.

Chris demonstrates many of the strengths of his archetype: a strong creative energy and enthusiasm, determination to convey what he experiences emotionally, a willing and open spirit, and a deep appreciation for the beauty around him. He seeks to communicate what he's feeling at the moment the shutter is snapped; like so many of his archetype, he finds himself in a relentless quest to get the message just right.

Chris very candidly shared a vulnerability of his archetype, the tendency to focus on his work to the exclusion of other important issues. His preoccupation with achieving perfection in his art, coupled with extended periods in "the zone" of his creative pursuit, impacted his personal life. He felt less successful as a husband and father than he wanted to be, and he learned that his obsession with creating could leave him depleted and in need of replenishment. For Chris, his family is the source for that important nourishment.

Another important lesson to be learned from the Creator's story is why it may be so challenging to manage individuals with this passion, especially if the leader of the individual does not share the same archetype. An essential aspect of leading successfully is being able to provide meaningful, actionable feedback, without demotivating the person to whom it's directed. With Chris Johns's story, we observe how closely connected people of this archetype are to their work. The work is not just an end product; it's an extension of their very being, a representation of their own journey. Therefore, it follows that for many of this archetype, criticizing their work is like criticizing who they are or finding fault with the life experiences that have shaped them. In Chris's case, the criticism early on in his career, while painful, was delivered by someone whose opinion mattered, a veteran photo editor who shares his same desire for quality. In guiding the work of a Creator, the feedback is important but so are the knowledge and background of the person delivering the message.

We see signs of the Discoverer archetype in Chris's determination to learn as much as possible about endangered animals like the cheetah. He and his crew spent weeks in the heat of Africa tracking the herd and studying the cheetahs' behaviors. Like a typical Discoverer, Chris was in search of the truth about these animals. The Altruist in him makes him want to make a difference in their fate by educating readers and encouraging the world to preserve the species for future generations.

One could argue that Chris struggles with another of the Creators' vulnerabilities: Creators sometimes become so immersed in the emotion of the moment that they ignore what logic would suggest as appropriate action. When encountering a female cheetah that broke away from her herd, someone less engaged with wildlife might have chosen to take cover, but Chris was so enthralled with the opportunity to make a connection that he chose to remain in the open. And what a gift he received from his willingness to stay put—an intimate exchange with an endangered species.

Native Americans believe that we all have a totem animal. For Chris Johns it must surely be the cheetah.

 SEVEN

The Discoverer

Profile Overview

Discoverers are the explorers and innovators of the organization. On a passionate quest to find a new treasure, be it a molecule to treat disease, the source of a buried ancient civilization, or the key to shifting consumer buying patterns, Discoverers thrive on the journey. They are especially adept at designing approaches (or experiments) that can help them uncover knowledge that can be processed in a way that provides new information leading to the next step in the journey or unveils a hidden truth.

Discoverers apply logic and linear thinking to assist in the planning necessary to carry out their discovery or achieve an innovation. Paradoxically, there is also strong capacity and comfort with the intuitive in some of the best Discoverers. Many of this archetype will describe a circumstance in which they arrived at a fork in the road where each avenue seemed equal, and it was through "gut" or intuition that they chose the path that led to their greatest discoveries. In these circumstances, the most capable of Discoverers is willing to relinquish their reliance on planning and linearity to allow their intuitive sense to inform the way forward toward the elusive "eureka moment." The combined characteristics of logic coupled with informed intuition allow this archetype to achieve breakthrough innovations and discoveries or solve challenging puzzles.

Discoverers are passionately curious and will tirelessly pursue exploration of an idea. They are often consumed with the solutions they seek, so much so that it commands their attention beyond all other activities. There are numerous stories of Discoverers who locked themselves away from others for weeks at a time while focusing on a particularly vexing problem, emerging only when the solution had been uncovered. As a general rule, this archetype is capable of intense focus and easily shuts out distractions around them. Because of this ability, many Discoverers can be perceived by others as aloof, disconnected, and uninterested in the well-being of others. In reality, actually the opposite may be true.

Discoverers thrive in an environment of intellectual stimulation and exploration. Therefore, organizations that rely on Discoverers would support their work by physically locating them in structures that facilitate communication with colleagues, provide them with access to research materials and tools, and provide them with the kind of collateral support that allows them to focus on their work with minimal distraction.

The passion that Discoverers have for information exchange and knowledge debate is supported by a culture that welcomes such interaction. In fact, this process of exchange is often the birthing ground of creative approaches to experimentation that lead to historic discoveries or innovations—beneficial by-products of the Discoverer's passion for processing knowledge.

Discoverers are usually lifelong knowledge seekers and avid learners. They are well aware of the large degree of information as yet unfathomed, which when available to them will lead to new insights about their chosen field of concentration. Seeking the unknown is the driver for this archetype. Discoverers operate with the belief that all information is readily available if the process to uncover it is well designed and they remain tenacious in their pursuit of the truth.

A particularly important characteristic of many Discoverers is their tendency to hold on to their beliefs or opinions about a particular topic of research interest but to be willing to change their opinions when compelling new information is uncovered. While Discoverers are generally thorough in their investigation of a topic and form their opinions only after careful research has yielded data to support their conclusions, in the face of new validated evidence or data, they will relinquish their formerly held beliefs in favor of new conclusions that can be drawn from the most recent information. Discoverers, in essence, function in a state of constant evolution, recognizing that today's conclusions may be upended by tomorrow's new discoveries. And it is, after all, the pursuit of the next new discovery or innovation that is the major driver for this archetype.

Characteristic Strengths

- Intense curiosity and passion for uncovering the unknown or the truth
- Passion for exploration and innovation
- Tenacity in pursuing information that can lead to solutions (sometimes described as "dogged determination")
- Ability to logically process data and draw useful conclusions
- Intense focus and ability to dive into their work
- Openness and receptivity to new valid information or research findings
- Passion for utilizing knowledge and learning to achieve new discoveries
- Great powers of observation
- Ability to utilize informed intuition to guide their work

Potential Vulnerabilities

- Sometimes succumb to tunnel vision and tune out everything else
- May be one-dimensional in their area of interest and miss opportunities to learn from other fields
- May sometimes become obsessive about the direction of their work and unable to realize when it is time to move on
- Can at times be consumed with the act of exploration rather than focused on the objective of achieving results

- May be perceived as disconnected from others or their surroundings

Leading and Managing the Discoverers

- Discoverers have an insatiable appetite for information. Their leaders have to be willing to freely exchange knowledge and insight with this archetype.
- The operative word for effectively managing Discoverers is "freedom." The leaders of this archetype must create an environment of freedom and, at the same time, provide enough structure to produce timely results.
- They work better with leaders who can match them step for step in their intensity, drive, and focus—leaders who are willing and able to engage in discussions about their progress, challenges, and triumphs.
- Discoverers can become consumed by the process of exploration and will at times venture in a direction solely based on curiosity. Effective leaders of this archetype are sure to keep them on track by examining results to confirm that additional research can be justified.
- Discoverers might find it hard to let go of an idea or a course of inquiry. However, this is an archetype that can be convinced to change course with sufficient evidence, information, and data that are substantially validated.
- Discoverers are so intense that they can seem preoccupied and obsessive about the issue they are trying to solve. They may carry around a puzzle they're trying to solve like another body appendage.
- They will resist taking on assignments that they perceive to be a distraction from the most important issue they are trying to resolve at the moment.
- One of the greatest forms of reward and recognition that can be given to Discoverers is direct credit, acknowledgment, and celebration of their contributions to their field.

- Discoverers thrive and depend on the creation and processing of knowledge. Providing such opportunities on a daily basis will keep them engaged and passionate about their work.

Examples of Roles or Functions in Which This Archetype Thrives

- Research science
- Archeology
- Astronomer
- Marketing research
- Sociologist
- Political scientist
- Investigative reporter
- Forensics
- Detective

Supportive Passion Profile Pairings

- **Processor.** Processors can provide great assistance to the work of Discoverers with the analysis of data and information derived from the research Discoverers conduct. This invaluable partnership allows Discoverers to make meaning of the information or evidence that they have gathered and to progress with their research.
- **Teacher.** Partnership with Teachers allows Discoverers to assure that their body of knowledge is shared with others. Teachers help others assimilate the knowledge generated through the work of Discoverers, and in doing so, they increase the probability that others will, in turn, contribute to the original body of knowledge created by Discoverers.
- **Conceiver.** The great passion of Conceivers is to examine a problem from multiple angles and arrive at a novel way to address or understand it. This partnership provides phenomenal support to Discoverers who consistently look for new ways to uncover the real truth (and the evidence to support it) within an issue or field of study.

Special Care Passion Profile Pairings

- **Builder.** The consistent drive and desire for achieving a vision, obtaining tangible results, taking risks, and advancing the business quickly that are so characteristic of Builders may result in friction with Discoverers who tend to advance in their work in a more measured and defined manner. Discoverers will most often look for evidence that indicates the way forward, while Builders will focus on their vision and create the way forward even in extremely ambiguous circumstances.

- **Transformer.** This passion archetype may exhibit the desire for change in an effort to disrupt the status quo. For the Discoverers who thrive in fact and evidence, making changes just for the sake of change itself often leaves them feeling frustrated and distracted from their work.

Archetype Examples

Jonas Salk.   Scientist, discoverer of the vaccine for polio

Bob Woodward and Carl Bernstein.   Investigative reporters for the *Washington Post* who uncovered the Watergate scandal during the administration of President Richard M. Nixon

Vincent Bugliosi.   Attorney, author, lead prosecutor of cult leader Charles Manson and his followers for murder

 The Discoverer's Story: Dr. P. Roy Vagelos

Primary profile.   *Discoverer*
Secondary profiles.   *Healer, Transformer*

At the age of 79, Roy Vagelos is one of the most passionate, purpose driven, and focused individuals we've ever met. He is at a time in his life when most individuals with his track record of accomplishment would be slowing down and basking in the rewards of a life well lived. But by all accounts, this physician and executive, the former CEO of the pharmaceutical giant Merck, has no intention of retiring. There are just too many things to do, too many goals to accomplish.

Roy Vagelos has had a stellar career as a physician, a scientist, and an executive. He started off on his journey to greatness with a coveted internship at Massachusetts General Hospital, followed by research positions at the National Institutes of Health and later Washington University before joining Merck in 1975. The son of Greek immigrants, Roy was born in Westfield, New Jersey, just a short drive from the then headquarters of the company that would be his home and his domain for nearly 20 exciting and productive years. It was, in fact, discussions with the scientists from Merck who frequented his father's restaurant that first piqued Roy's interest in chemistry. These scientists seemed to be doing exciting work that made a difference in the lives of millions, and Roy wanted in on the fun.

"My brain is scientific, and I love interacting with scientists," Roy told us. "Discovery is the most important thing in my life. The thrill for me has been the identification of something new that can change the future, whether it was through the basic research that I did at the university or taking my lipid knowledge to Merck and making cholesterol lowering compounds."

Beginning his career with Merck as the head of basic research, Roy progressed to president of the Merck Research Laboratories and later to the top job, where he led the company to seven consecutive years as *Fortune's* Most Admired Company. Under his leadership, Merck produced a string of blockbuster products, developing drug therapies to treat conditions such as high cholesterol, hepatitis B, arthritis, glaucoma, bacterial infections, and ulcers.

Roy led the groundbreaking research through which lovastatin and simvastatin were discovered. These two medicines decrease blood cholesterol by inhibiting an enzyme (HMG CoA reductase) that is instrumental in directing the carbon in our diets to cholesterol synthesis. He also fundamentally reshaped the perception of pharmaceutical company greed by guiding Merck through a complex international bureaucratic process that resulted in the unprecedented donation of Mectizan—a product that treats river blindness, a widespread and debilitating disease that is endemic in Africa and Central America. In a bold move that has since cost the company over $3.2 billion in tablets and $30 million in direct financial support, Merck committed to providing Mectizan free of charge to anyone who needs it anywhere in the world—for as long as it is needed.

At the time this commitment was made, Roy knew that 18 million people were infected with the parasite that causes river blindness and that 80 million more were at risk. He also knew that the patients who desperately needed the medicine could least afford to pay for it. Merck scientists had discovered an effective prevention for this terrible disease, and the Healer in Roy was determined to see that it got to those who needed it most. This pivotal decision not only made a positive difference for whole villages in Africa and Central America but it also won the hearts and minds of Merck employees around the globe. It also made Merck a virtual magnet for the very best talent available, facilitating the recruitment of additional brilliant minds to an organization with already considerable bench strength.

But Roy at his core is a Discoverer, with a passion to uncover new information and knowledge that can be brought to bear on complex challenges and improve human health. Early on in his research, he described himself as "obsessed with the desire to understand the metabolism of lipids." These are the fats that our bodies utilize in vital organs like the brain, forms of which can also be detrimental to our health by creating plaques that clog vessels and lead to heart disease. It was that obsession that drove Roy to substantially change the drug discovery process at Merck. Instead of the shotgun method of screening large numbers of compounds through animal studies to uncover potential new products, Roy felt strongly that a more precise approach should be utilized.

His understanding of the discovery process led Roy to champion biochemical targeting as a means to identifying new drug candidates. With this methodology, a team of scientists under his leadership eventually discovered a novel substance for lowering blood cholesterol that became the bestseller Zocor. However, the path to discovering this blockbuster was not easy; Roy was up against a number of challenges.

First, he was fighting resistance to his ideas about the drug discovery process, in large part because his style of biochemistry and enzymology were relatively new at the time. This was further complicated by the fact that although Roy was at the helm of the research laboratories, he had never himself discovered a drug. So he became engaged in an uphill battle to transform an organization that had been successful in an industry where it (and most of its competitors) was exclusively screening for compounds using animal models of disease.

Working in his favor at the time was the culture that Roy had begun to foster in the laboratories. Structured much like a university campus, the labs were located on the same site as the marketing and corporate offices at the Rahway, New Jersey, location, where scientists could easily exchange ideas and debate issues with one another and their marketing colleagues. It was a perfect environment for the Discoverer in Roy who, as head of research, was intimately involved with every important project that was underway. He was both insatiable in his curiosity and tenacious in his pursuit of answers, often pulling aside both senior and junior scientists (whom he encountered when strolling down the halls of the research buildings) to inquire about the results of the latest experiment or give advice on an approach that he thought might yield more information. "It's my life to be able to work out problems," he told us.

And work them out, he would. But first Roy needed to transform the research process so that Merck could outdistance its competitors in the race for new blockbuster products. "I came into the company with the idea that it should be among the best in the world, but I needed to figure out where it was and have a plan for changing it," said Roy. "I learned we had a weakness [in the drug discovery process] that was hurting the organization. Even before coming into the industry, I thought that there must be a better way to do things. So when I met with Henry Gadsden [then CEO of Merck] during my recruitment process, I told him that I wanted to change the way we went about drug discovery and use a more scientifically rational process. When I asked if he would mind, Henry told me, 'If we didn't want change around here, we wouldn't be hiring you.'"

Over time, the combination of Roy's intense interest in every program, his keen insight about how to keep scientists focused on producing results, and his ability to spot a winning project paid off. Roy was successful in persuading researchers to change their approach to drug discovery and adopt his biochemical targeting methodology. Without this single accomplishment, many of the breakthrough products that were hallmarks of his tenure might never have been discovered.

In the years since his exciting time at Merck, Roy Vagelos has remained equally intense and driven. He is now the chairman of two small pharmaceutical companies (Regeneron Pharmaceuticals and Theravance Corporation), and he works with Columbia Medical Center educating doctors—all with the energy and enthusiasm for hard work of a man half his age. "I don't know what passion is," he told us, "other than the enthusiasm and a deep interest in carrying out a job." With increasing animation, he went on to explain: "Passion is transmitted enthusiasm that impacts other people, . . . and it's almost infectious. I believe that passionate people are driven in what they do and experience joy in accomplishment. So I would rather work with them than take trips or be on a cruise. At this point in my life, I could do lots of other things, but I keep being drawn back to medicine and research. This is where I know I can make a difference."

⊕→ Profile Analysis

Like many individuals who carry the Discoverer archetype, Roy Vagelos admits to being consumed and obsessed when working through a difficult problem. He spent a large portion of his research career working out the metabolism of lipids, and in doing so, he contributed to the discovery of compounds that save millions of lives each year. To do this required a constant attention to the problem and an unwavering focus on the objective. Typical of a Discoverer, Roy doggedly pursued a solution to cholesterol management until the labs developed one, which in turn only sparked his desire to create the next generation of new products. An ongoing quest for innovation and new knowledge was a hallmark of his leadership style.

For Roy, science and discovery are the fuels that feed his body, the air that he breathes in, the elixir for his very survival. He is a man of both passion and curiosity coupled with the drive to put his discoveries to good use. When he enters a room, people feel that passion and experience his intensity as a palpable gravitational force that pulls others toward him. In this respect he defies the stereotypical image of the lone scientist working in his laboratory with little connection to the outer world. Instead, Roy thrives on exchanging ideas, debating the science, and challenging himself and others to develop innovative solutions to serious diseases.

It is his Healer passion that has allowed Roy to avoid two vulnerabilities of Discoverers, which are to sometimes be consumed with the process of exploration without maintaining a focus on achieving results that can be practically applied, and to sometimes be unable to realize when an avenue of research has been exhausted and it's time to move on. Healers want to make a difference and alleviate suffering, so Roy's focus when working with scientists under his direction was to keep them on a track that would lead to solutions. He both logically and intuitively understood when enough effort had been invested in a project that was unlikely to yield useful results. Therefore, during his tenure, he was able to shift the efforts of researchers to more productive directions, resulting in Merck's enviable product pipeline.

As a Healer, Roy took to heart the guiding principle of company founder George Merck to "remember to put patients first," sure that in doing so the profits would follow. Without this as a tenet of his leadership, the company would not have contributed to the fight to eradicate river blindness or supported the development of a number of "orphan drugs" to treat rare diseases in a limited patient population. Despite the financial investment required to take these actions, the Healer in Roy saw it as a moral imperative.

Finally, we see Roy's Transformer passion play an important part in his ability to achieve a dramatic change in the drug discovery process at Merck. Without the innate comfort with change so typical of

Transformers and without an accompanying desire to help others embrace a new approach to research, many of the company's achievements in product development might not have been possible—or they would most certainly have taken longer to reach fruition. Indeed, a hallmark of Roy's leadership style was his constant search for a better way to accomplish goals . . . a new way to seek out solutions. He often examined the organization and compared it to a set standard—one of absolute excellence. His goal as a leader was to continually transform the organization to achieve a new level of excellence that set the benchmark to which others could aspire.

And with change as an abiding constant in his life, the Transformer passion continues to serve Roy well, as he reinvents himself in these years after Merck. It is this passion, which has triumphed over the complacency that might have set in upon "retirement," that will allow the son of poor Greek immigrants, who came to lead one of the most successful companies in the world, to continue to create more magic in his life and work in the years ahead.

 EIGHT

The Processor

Profile Overview

Processors make up the spinal column of the organization—they are
the sustainers of structure, function, and tradition. Without them,
the organization will struggle with developing systems that help
accomplish goals and will risk losing sight of its history and institutional wisdom. The Processors help the organization prepare adequately for anticipated changes or potential problems and execute
its plans with success.

Processors are highly quality oriented, and they serve the organization by establishing and maintaining quality standards. Whether
the standard relates to the manufacture of a product, the development
of internal accounting systems, or an orderly emergency evacuation
plan, the Processors value quality and strive to consistently deliver it
in a cost-efficient way.

Many Processors are highly analytical, and they enjoy sifting
through data or information to see what it reveals. Their passion for
analysis and order allows Processors to wade through volumes of data
that would be staggering for other archetypes, and it enables them to
create internal systems or decision processes to support the organiza-

tion. The gifts of this archetype are the Processors' abilities to recognize patterns in data and identify relevant connections as they relate to the context of an issue they are analyzing, while setting aside data that may not have direct bearing on the situation at hand. The pleasure they take in diving into the details of an issue allows the Processors to use analysis and synthesis of information to provide direction, take action, or deliver valuable assistance to others.

Because of their passion for creating work structure, Processors are excellent at executing prescribed plans, which many of this archetype accomplish flawlessly. They can be counted on for their reliability, and they will work consistently to get their assignments completed on time and within budget. This talented archetype can examine a plan and rapidly understand all of the complexities of the systems or procedures that will be necessary to achieve desired goals. They will define the explicit step-by-step process necessary to take the plan from concept to reality. Because they are also realistic and practical, Processors are likely to correctly identify the expected time or financial investment that would be required to achieve the plan, even when others may be more optimistic about the requirements.

The practicality of Processors serves them well, as they plan for the inevitable pitfalls that plague any project or activity and put systems in place to manage them. With a passion to make things operate efficiently and effectively, this is an archetype that, with data in hand, will look ahead to determine how the current information will impact the ability of the organization to function well in the future. When a pitfall is encountered, the talented Processor will calmly and effectively provide the direction that can guide others through the difficulty.

Processors may encounter challenges when they work with others who are not equally quality oriented. Because they can be perfectionists, some Processors find it difficult to relax their standards for how work gets accomplished, even when those standards are well in excess of what is truly necessary.

Other archetypes with whom Processors will work may well be comfortable with ambiguity and limited concrete data with which to make decisions. Working with such archetypes may be a challenge for data-focused Processors who seek complete information upon which to base decisions. With rapidly changing and competitive business decisions on the daily menu of most organizations, Processors will be faced with walking the fine line of uncovering enough information to help set direction and prevent disaster, while leaving sufficient flexibility in their approach to allow the organization to be nimble.

Characteristic Strengths

- Passion for analysis
- Ability to identify the data most relevant to the situation at hand
- Highly quality oriented
- Strong organizational abilities
- Very detail oriented
- Able to anticipate how impending challenges might affect the success of the organization or a mission and plan for managing the challenges
- Excellent at building systems or processes that can help others manage the business, especially during times of difficulty
- Highly practical and realistic in their approach to business issues
- Reliable implementers of established plans

Potential Vulnerabilities

- Can be indiscriminate perfectionists
- At times unyielding about detouring from established processes or procedures, even when it is beneficial to do so
- Can be tied to tradition, even when current evidence suggests that change is necessary
- May set standards that are so high that others find it impossible to meet them
- May find it difficult to work in rapidly changing ambiguous environments where data to support decision making are minimal

Leading and Managing the Processors

- They thrive in a structured environment, so place them in a situation with well-defined structure or provide them with the latitude to create the structure that's needed.

- They are a go-to archetype when you want to create order out of chaos.

- Processors are often a great source of institutional history and will recollect facts and figures from the past with ease.

- Clarity of procedures, expectations, and deadlines is essential to their success. Provide them with direction that includes these elements.

- Processors are more uncomfortable with ambiguity than are other archetypes. Work with them to identify the concrete aspects of a situation to which they can anchor.

- You may need to be the vision holder for Processors because they may be focused on details and precision at the expense of achieving a larger objective.

- Managing the relationships that Processors develop with those who don't share their passion for precision can be an issue. Because Processors may view others as being sloppy and disorganized, they may discount their input.

- Be patient and appreciative of the depth of detail Processors will undoubtedly want to share with you. Don't glaze over when hearing the details and miss the important observations that may make a difference in the business.

- Processors are driven by facts, numbers, and detailed information, but they may lack lateral vision.

- You may need to be careful what you ask Processors to do because they will do it—sometimes without sufficiently challenging the directive.

- They may initially be resistant to change, but they are an important ally in successfully accomplishing it. Don't leave Processors out of a change initiative.

- Remember to reward Processors within organizational guidelines. They will be acutely aware of their performance relative to the compensation policy.
- Many Processors take pride in their commitment to the organization. Recognitions such as service awards are not to be overlooked or minimized in importance with this archetype.

Examples of Roles or Functions in Which This Archetype Thrives

- Accounting
- Information technology
- Manufacturing
- Six Sigma team
- Attorney (especially corporate counsel or litigation)
- Engineering
- Systems analyst
- Compensation and benefits specialist
- Air traffic controller
- Pilot

Supportive Passion Profile Pairings

- **Transformer.** The Transformers recognize the need to bring others along in a change initiative and will reach out to the Processors for support and assistance in developing systems to sustain change.
- **Teacher.** Teachers will appreciate the systems and analysis that the Processors help to develop because the Teachers can use that information and knowledge to share with others to promote learning.
- **Discoverer.** Discoverers depend on the detailed analysis that Processors provide to help discern fact from fiction and uncover truth.
- **Healer.** Healers can serve as allies to Processors who may find themselves otherwise marginalized in group situations. Healers will appreciate their value and assist others in doing the same.

Special Care Passion Profile Pairings

- **Builder.**   While Builders can often benefit from the disciplined passion of the Processor archetype, the degree of time and attention that some Processors give to information and data analysis can at times impede the Builders' desire for rapid results. This can cause friction between the two archetypes. Yet the Processors' appetite for analysis is often beneficial when there is a need for the kind of detailed planning that the Builders would ordinarily move through too quickly.

- **Altruist.**   Altruists can become focused on providing resources to those less fortunate beyond the point where they should be required to stand on their own, and doing so may conflict with the Processors' more frugal tendencies.

- **Creator.**   People of this archetype often operate best in limited structure, and Creators may resist the structure that Processors wish to establish. Consequently, Creators may push against the Processors' practical tendencies.

- **Conceiver.**   This is an archetype that does not think linearly, which may be difficult for Processors to understand.

Archetype Examples

Peter Orszag.   Head of the U.S. Office of Management and Budget

Paul Volcker.   Former chairman of the U.S. Federal Reserve

Bill Smith.   Motorola engineer, one of the creators of the Six Sigma quality management process

Captain Chesley "Sully" Sullenberger.   Successfully landed USAir flight 1549 on the Hudson River in New York, saving the lives of 155 people

 ## The Processor's Story: Commander Gregory McWherter

Primary profile.   *Processor*

Secondary profiles.   *Teacher, Healer*

O n a starless night in the dead of winter, Greg McWherter found himself flying an F/A-18 Hornet fighter jet off the coast of Australia in the worst possible conditions. Visibility was at zero, and Greg's body was being assaulted with 7G forces that would make the average person pass out at the controls of this $18 million beast—yet he not only had to fly it but he also had to land it on an aircraft carrier waiting somewhere below.

Greg circled in search of the ship and decreased his altitude, still trying to find his way through the soup, as one of his sensors sounded an alarm. He had to manage a multifunction instrument panel, with seemingly hundreds of data points coming at him at once, and he could hear voices from ground control and his remote wingman talking to him on the radio. Discerning the alarms and voices to pay attention to from those to ignore for the moment was crucial.

Looking below, he finally spotted the carrier. The seas were so rough that waves were washing over the deck. One pass over the ship and he knew landing wouldn't be easy. But he circled back around again, sighted the landing lights, and managed to snag the plane's tail hook into the arresting wire on the deck and land the plane. As he listened to the engines wind down, Greg quietly chuckled to himself about the Navy's uncanny ability to pick any 500-mile radius, find the worst possible weather in it, and put an aircraft carrier there on which some poor sucker had to land.

Greg McWherter is no ordinary pilot. He's a former Top Gun instructor who has spent the bulk of his career flying from aircraft carriers, and he is now the commanding officer and flight leader of the elite Blue Angels—the world's oldest and most renowned flight demonstration squadron, based at the Naval Air Station in Pensacola, Florida. For Greg, that night in the milky skies over an unforgiving sea was just another day at the office.

This glamorous, testosterone-saturated world, the stuff from which movies are made, was the seduction that attracted Greg to a career in military aviation from the time he entered college at The Citadel. There he found himself at an ROTC orientation with 200 other students, all of whom had seen the movie *Top Gun* and most of whom raised their hands when asked if they wanted to be pilots. They were told that com-petition was tough and that the Navy allotted only one slot per year to a Citadel graduate. To be selected, they'd have to be the best in their class and have a technical major. Greg decided that spot would be his.

No stranger to hard work, Greg grew up in what he describes as a "structured household" in which he was required to always have a plan and something constructive to do. "It's an environment in which I thrive," he told us. The military is also an environment that some of the young recruits he now trains find challenging to accept. "A lot of kids today don't have structure in their family unit, so they see the structure [required to serve in the military] as inhibiting personal growth. I see it as just the opposite," Greg noted.

Much of his work in shaping young sailors is defined by Greg's use of structure and support systems to help transform new recruits into capa-ble leaders. "In the military it's all about structure and planning," he said. "The flight schedule dictates what we do. We have a thousand parts that need to move together in unison, and we need to do it on a daily basis."

When examining the grueling schedule of the Blue Angels, it's clear why structure is so critical to their success. They perform at 35 air show sites across the country and in Canada, spend 250 to 300 days a year on the road, and fly six times per week—every week of the year. With 12- to 14-hour days and only Mondays off, it's an environment where the time clock reigns supreme. Unlike other operational forces, the maintenance team preps the jets and conducts final inspections before each flight so that the pilots can walk out of the briefing room and directly into the cockpits. This is a team that is built on trust, where structure supplies the framework through which everyone can learn to perform their job flawlessly. "If we don't do well, people get hurt—or worse," said Greg.

Making split-second decisions based on a multitude of information coming from the instrument cluster is a constant occurrence when at the helm of a fighter jet. When individuals come out of the Fleet Replace-ment Squadron, they know the very basics of how to fly and handle the plane in a combat situation, but they are unprepared for the amount of information they must manage in a real battle situation or when flying precision drills like those of the Blue Angels. But for Greg, information is a real passion. "I personally like being able to process more and more information at once. However, when pilots first came to work for me on an aircraft carrier, we actually needed to limit the amount of information coming at them, so we'd turn off some of the cockpit boxes until they learned to process information in greater volume," said Greg.

Ultimately, the objective is to have pilots comfortable with processing multiple data points, even in a crisis situation. Expanding their bandwidth for data management can mean the difference between life and death, so the Navy educates pilots on crew resource management (CRM) to enable them to deal with challenges in the cockpit. "When flying aircraft off a carrier, you begin to realize that you're all alone, even though it looks like you have outside help," Greg reflected. "So we're teaching pilots to use all available resources to solve problems in the cockpit before reaching out for help. They're trained for the worst-case scenario. That means that they have memorized certain procedures to deal with emergencies and are acting on them. The engine fire, flight control malfunctions, or the ground rushing up at 600 knots—these are not going to wait for you to call your buddy! In short, CRM is a must in our business but not to the extent that it paralyzes our ability to make decisions and act in a timely manner."

Even at Top Gun school, pilots are trained to be acutely aware of every moment of a flight. Where most units debrief by reviewing the video of the flight once the pilots have landed, when Greg taught at Top Gun, he would first require pilots to recite the experience from memory. They would then compare their recollections to actual video footage to confirm its accuracy. Greg believes this practice develops more capable pilots who learn how to absorb information in crisis situations and think through alternatives critical to their survival. "But if we're going to teach them how to think and how to lead, we have to start early," he observed.

From Greg's perspective, most young recruits come into the service with few marketable skills. Some may have just finished high school, and a few may have obtained an advanced degree. "We put them on a ship for six months, we don't pay them well, the food isn't that great, and the working conditions are not the best. At the same time we have to motivate them, . . . which I really don't think is hard to do," said Greg. Despite such working conditions, Greg has developed high-functioning teams by taking a keen interest in each person under his command. "You have to show them that you care deeply about them and are looking out for their best interest. That keeps them motivated, and the news that you care spreads like wildfire," he said.

Consistent and regular communication is the primary process that Greg uses to keep the squadron motivated. While some military leaders use formal meetings (called "Quarters") as the only means of communication, Greg believes in managing by walking around—and *he* takes it seriously. A timer on his computer will turn yellow if it's been two days since he's visited a division under his command and red if it's been four days since he's done so. "I make sure that I make the rounds to every shop in my squadron," Greg explained. "I want to be sure that they're getting everything that they need to do their jobs and everything they need for their own development. I sit and talk with them to find out what's on their minds, what they might be struggling with, and I encourage them to keep learning." Since Greg visits regularly, the squadron knows that he's not just checking off the box on a list of daily duties but truly cares about their well-being.

Surprisingly, the squadron operates much like a democracy because Greg also works to push decision making down to the lowest level. In most meetings, decisions are voted on by all officers with equal weight, except those that relate to safety or personnel issues, where Greg's opinion takes precedence. The squadron is a tightly knit team in which members learn early on that the team is more important than the individual. Its culture is marked by Greg's perspective on his role as commander. "I tell my folks that the Navy is not paying me to fly aircraft; they're paying me to develop the next generation of leaders," said Greg. "And the first step to becoming a great leader is to become a good teammate."

It's hard not to be impressed with the team that Greg is leading. The Blue Angels is a professional, fit, courageous, and courteous squadron. When meeting them, you sense that they're anything but ordinary, despite the fact that they all insist that they're no more important than any other unit. As commander, Greg would like to leave a leadership legacy where people have benefited as much from the interaction with him as he has in working with them. Ultimately, he wants to build a squadron of leaders that are stronger than when he arrived. We think it's one more goal that he's well on the way to achieving.

→ Profile Analysis

Greg McWherter's leadership accomplishments are an example of the power of the mosaic of his passions. He capitalized on his Processor passion to move fluidly through the rigorous structure characteristic of military environments, and he utilized that structure as a platform for his own learning and development, which have continued throughout his career.

A passionate Processor, Greg has developed systems for helping others learn. While personally being able to manage large volumes of data in dangerous situations, Greg was aware that teaching others to do so would require a system that could help them develop this competency. We see him apply such a system with pilots at Top Gun and with pilots new to the aircraft carrier environment. At Top Gun, his practice of having pilots debrief from memory helped the pilots learn to be very much in the moment while at the controls. "Initially," he said "it slowed down their flying progress because they were concentrating on absorbing everything going on around them. But after a time, they became even more effective pilots."

While instructing young pilots in the aircraft carrier fleet, rather than flooding them with information, Greg shut off cockpit boxes that were not absolutely essential. He then added them back as pilots became more comfortable with the equipment and the environment. In this way, he was able to build a highly competent team using his passion for systems and structure as the vehicle.

Further evidence of Greg's Processor passion is observed in his excitement about managing large volumes of data. He enjoys challenging himself with increasing amounts of information to see just how much he can process at once. That passion has no doubt served him well in the cockpit, especially in poor flying conditions or during battle situations.

Greg's Teacher passion manifests in his keen interest in the development of members of his squadron. He takes time to mentor other members of the team and is consistent about setting aside structured time for communication and sharing. Once again, the Processor passion for creating systems to support his efforts to develop his team is evident in Greg's color-coded reminders for visiting each shop in the squadron on a routine basis. However, his concern about the quality of life for those under his command extends beyond a cursory fulfillment of his duties as a military leader. Greg is also a Healer who cares deeply about everyone under his command and often takes home their problems as his own until a solution is found. The Healer passion infuses Greg with a sense of personal responsibility for others' challenges—be it for the pilot struggling on the job or the maintenance technician dealing with a family illness.

NINE

The Transformer

CHANGE IS THE PROCESS BY WHICH
THE FUTURE INVADES OUR LIVES.
—ALVIN TOFFLER

Profile Overview

Transformers are the alchemists and change agents of the organization. They identify and embrace possibilities for improvement in the business, the environment, themselves, and others, and they are passionate about working to accomplish the change. More than just seeing possibilities, this archetype can see the full potential of what can be, and they will eagerly gravitate toward it.

Transformers also demonstrate a great willingness to let go. They are comfortable with venturing into new territory, releasing their hold on tradition, and seeking new and better ways of doing things. In fact, their passion often drives Transformers to look for ways to change existing systems because the act of making change happen, for Transformers, is an act of manifesting possibility. Rather than waiting for change to occur organically, Transformers are driven to orchestrate it in part because they become bored when things remain the same for too long.

In their personal or professional lives, change remains the seduction for this archetype. Transformers, for example, may insist on an adventurous new vacation experience rather than visiting the same place each year. They may easily reinvent themselves when they find it is time to do so, seeking new ways to apply their talents or new applications for their interests. At the same time, this archetype will look at an existing business system that others feel is working well and ask: "How can it be improved? How can we get better results? Do we even need this system at all?" Transformers are willing to ask the tough questions and adopt a controversial and courageous position when they believe the current process, system, or way of doing business is no longer serving the organization well. For this archetype, everything is open to scrutiny and may be a candidate for change. Whether it is as complex as the reorchestration of a business or as personal as rearranging the surroundings in their homes, Transformers gravitate toward the new and improved in form, function, and results.

The challenges Transformers face are significant, especially when they are trying to influence others. This archetype can clearly envision the final state that they are working toward, but they also have a driving need to help others share the same vision. As a result, they are often tasked with helping others overcome their own fear and resistance to change. To do so successfully, gifted Transformers are capable of freely traveling between various dimensions of thought, including their own view of the desired state, the worldview of others who may be struggling with the change, and the cultural view of the organization as a whole. The most passionate of Transformers are able to fully immerse themselves in each dimension so that they can deeply understand their own motivations and the underlying motivations and concerns of others. They also understand how to stimulate a shift in the organizational culture so that it becomes more open, accepting, and enthusiastic about the new direction.

It is not enough for the Transformers to set off alone on a new course; they are passionate about taking others along on the journey. This is an archetype of master painters who develop the picture for others, creating a compelling case for change and growth. But knowing just which colors to choose and where to make the first brushstroke on the canvas is the true gift of the Transformers. They examine and dissect how the individuals around them are processing information about an impending change and then structure messages that resonate with others, so that they can create an opening through which the change can be examined with minimal fear and resistance. In this way, the painting on the canvas begins to take shape for others and moves from abstraction to impressionism, where the clear outline of the new destination can be seen and indeed appreciated.

Characteristic Strengths

- Passion for change and improvement
- Comfort with ambiguity
- Strong sense of adventure
- Willingness to delve into the unknown
- Courageously share their views about what needs to change
- Outstanding ability to identify the levers that might help others embrace a new direction
- Superior ability to identify potential
- Can work well with a skeleton plan and will then fill in the blanks
- Engender trust from others
- Create positive emotional energy

Potential Vulnerabilities

- May promote nonessential changes to reduce their own boredom with the status quo
- Can sometimes become impatient with others who do not readily embrace a new direction
- May struggle with developing a structure through which a change can be initiated
- Can sometimes push change too rapidly and exclude others in the process
- When disengaging too quickly from the past, may overlook the valuable lessons learned

Leading and Managing the Transformers

- The most beneficial support that a leader of Transformers can give is a clear vision of the desired state. Transformers will firmly imprint this vision and work tirelessly with others to make it a reality.
- This archetype is best assigned to positions where change is imminent or ongoing—they thrive in jobs where chaos reigns supreme.
- Transformers may want to accomplish change too quickly and may mistake compliance in others with commitment to the goal. Transformers will do a fine job of communicating the goal to others, but they sometimes fail to include others in designing how it will be achieved.
- Transformers may need help to establish a process with milestones to measure progress to prevent undertaking too many complex activities simultaneously.
- Transformers may need assistance with identifying signs of organizational readiness for change.
- The greatest injustice any leader can be guilty of when managing Transformers is in asking them to orchestrate change without providing them the support they need to be successful.
- When giving assignments where rapid change is likely, frequent feedback and contact is critical so the Transformers keep the leader abreast of progress and the leader has an opportunity to correct the course as needed.
- Transformers enjoy being a part of the new environment that their work has created. Giving them an opportunity to take a leadership role in the changed environment is a prized reward and the ultimate form of recognition for a job well done.

Examples of Roles or Functions in Which This Archetype Thrives

- Mergers and acquisitions teams
- Major change project teams
- Large-scale reorganization projects

- Planning for sustainability
- Redesign projects
- Performance improvement teams
- Political leadership
- Nongovernmental organizations (NGOs) working on issues such as global warming, world health, and education reforms
- Any leadership position in which spearheading change is essential

Supportive Passion Profile Pairings

- **Processor.** Processors support Transformers by helping to establish much-needed systems for managing the change they seek to initiate.
- **Connector.** Connectors assist Transformers with navigating through tricky political situations; they help to identify individuals whose support will be essential for resolving change issues; and they may act as diplomats on behalf of the Transformers.
- **Healer.** Healers provide vital support to Transformers as they seek to orchestrate change, which invariably impacts the culture and morale of the organization. Healers can serve as barometers for the pain and fear others in the organization are experiencing, and they can assist Transformers with helping the reluctant people to embrace the change.

Special Care Passion Profile Pairings

- **Altruist.** Altruists have a tendency to provide support to others when they should have achieved the ability to stand on their own. When paired with Transformers who are undertaking large-scale change projects, Altruists may advocate for greater tolerance and patience with those in key positions who should be fully supporting the new direction but are not. This advocacy, if embraced by Transformers, may slow down or derail the project's success. If resisted by Transformers, the advocacy of the Altruist may be a source of contention and discord.
- **Teacher.** Change processes frequently cause a disruption in the flow of knowledge and assimilation of information as rapid ad-

justments to the way work gets accomplished are implemented. This may frustrate or alienate the Teachers, or it may leave them feeling unneeded or undervalued.

Archetype Examples

Barack Obama.   Forty-fourth U.S. president, former community organizer

Nelson Mandela.   Former president of South Africa, Nobel Peace Prize winner

 ## The Transformer's Story: Philip J. Schoonover

Primary profile.   *Transformer*
Secondary profiles.   *Altruist, Teacher*

There are times when even passionate leaders can fail, especially if they succumb to the vulnerabilities of those passions. Phil Schoonover is one such leader. Surprisingly humble and candid about his shortcomings, Phil is a self-proclaimed survivor of multiple business near-death experiences. When we sat down to speak with him, he was walking through the characteristic long tunnel of another, hoping that the light at the end of it wasn't that of an oncoming train. As the chairman and CEO of Circuit City Stores, based in Richmond, Virginia, Phil was in the fight of his life to save and transform this consumer electronics retailer.

Business hadn't always been that tough. In the first 24 months of his tenure, Phil's transformation plan for an ailing Circuit City resulted in a stock value increase from $14.50 to $32.50 and a doubling of the company's market share in the digital television sector. Under his leadership, Circuit City also built a $300 million services business, and it grew its Web-based business from $300 million to $1.4 billion. Things were looking up, and Wall Street had begun to think that there might be hope for this struggling brand. Management's plan to win in the home entertainment and digital home services business, while becoming a multichannel retailer, seemed to be working.

Having worked for Best Buy (as well as Sony and TOPS Appliance City) prior to taking the helm at Circuit City, Phil learned about change at the knee of retail giants, and he developed his own understanding of how to make change happen. In Phil's early years at Sony in the 1980s, he cut his teeth on a major business transformation that repositioned the organization from a manufacturing and research company to one of the greatest brands of the decade. At the age of 27, Phil was fast-tracked into the executive ranks and became the youngest vice president in Sony's history, an accomplishment for which he offers much credit to the mentors and teachers who helped him along the way. "Sony was in a massive growth phase," he told us. "We went from $1 billion in sales to $20 billion in sales in just nine years. And we did it by building a high-quality culture and pulling the business together in all arenas." In Phil's opinion, the magic of transforming a large organization rests not just in the metrics, the architecture, and the number crunching but also in the engagement of the minds, passions, and skills of employees. It's a lesson that he learned in the early years at Sony and a task for which he assumed personal responsibility at Circuit City.

Things changed dramatically in the autumn of 2006 when Circuit City experienced the perfect storm. Electronic retailer rivals Best Buy, Wal-Mart, and Amazon.com were hammering it in the marketplace and were chipping away at the company's performance during the critical holiday buying season. Reflecting on this challenging season, Phil told us, "Life throws you curves, but I've never lost hope for a better day." This was not the first time that he'd been up against tough challenges, and with 43,000 employees counting on him to turn things around, Phil Schoonover's optimism became a critical ally in an otherwise daunting business environment. But would it and his ambitious plans for transforming the business be enough? Could he turn things around quickly enough?

Typical of a Transformer, Phil spent a good deal of his time working to communicate his vision for the company by engaging employees through town hall meetings, workshops, and smaller meetings with selected individuals. "I use the head, heart, and hands model. For the 'head' portion of the model, I appeal to the logic of things (Does the plan make sense?) and spend a fair amount of time communicating our strategy." For the "heart" piece, Phil uses a variety of tools to connect employees at their core with the work that they do. "When we lose ground, I find it's the 'heart' piece we haven't paid enough attention to," he told us. And the "hands" portion of the engagement model has been addressed through investments that Circuit City has made in training its employees. Even top executives like Phil were expected to facilitate training programs. Among the members of the leadership team, taking responsibility and delivering on commitments was key. "I hold myself accountable, and I like to keep it real," Phil said. "When we're successful, we celebrate with our employees. But I also expected them to tell us when we suck."

Never was this system of workforce engagement more important than in the months following the wall the company hit in 2006. Despite a number of business improvements instituted under Phil's leadership—including launching a new Web site, introducing a new service culture, and creating a company strategy that was a win-win for customers, associates (employees), and shareholders—the enthusiasm and promise that he'd worked to build in the organization were impacted by the beating the company took from its competitors. With associates becoming negative and discouraged, Phil knew he was facing an issue that he needed to remedy at once. Approaching the problem with his usual candor, he called together employees to deliver one important message: "I told our associates that Amazon wasn't here 10 years ago, yet we're a 50-year-old business," he said. "We've doubled the services business in the last 3 years, so we should gain confidence from this, rather than be discouraged. I told them I'd like people at the individual level to play to win."

Despite his actions to rally the troops internally, Circuit City's stock price continued to slide as it lost market share to competitors. This was a situation that Phil realized would require the company to cycle faster than planned and move from incremental change to a massive transformation process. Significant costs needed to be permanently removed from the business if things were to turn around, so following the dismal holiday season performance, Circuit City let go 3,400 of its most experienced workers in March 2007. The company likely cut more than headcount; in the process, they lost a great deal of institutional wisdom and history.

In order to make the most of cost reductions, management understood that employees would need to learn a new way to work. So every process from scheduling to unloading a truck was revamped, and 40,000 employees were retrained. While these bold initiatives were successful in the elimination of $200 million in selling, general, and administrative costs, Phil says the company lost its selling culture in the process. With a growth platform that was centered in customer service, the company's future survival was in dangerous territory.

Phil was reflective when asked how he weathered the constant uphill battle of transforming the company. "Listen, the problems that Circuit City faces today were not created just a few months ago. A series of decisions made over the years is what led us to where we are. This [situation] took a decade to evolve. We're doing the right things; what we need now is time."

Unfortunately, time was running out. There was pressure from shareholders that resulted in a proxy battle with Wattles Capital Management that eventually led to Blockbuster making an offer to buy the company. During a critical period of the transformation, management became distracted with examining strategic alternatives, and associates became fearful that their jobs would disappear. This combination of events and decisions resulted in a death spiral that Circuit City did not survive.

Other problems contributed to the failure of Phil's transformation plan. He acknowledged that management had asked employees for too much too quickly. In doing so, they had contributed to the cultural shift away from selling, and employees' time and attention became centered on processes rather than serving customers. To address the issue, management took action by changing the compensation package to keep associates motivated. They revised internal scorecards to emphasize customer service and provided store associates with point-of-service handheld computers. In addition, Phil and his management team met with every single store director for open dialogues and town hall meetings. "We admitted our mistakes to them," Phil shared. "We realized that we had to make the people doing the work part of the plan. In fact, we needed them to become evangelists *for* the plan. And we realized that while we needed to get $200 million out of our cost basis, we also needed to build a selling culture; these objectives don't have to be mutually exclusive."

When reflecting on this period of his career, Phil admitted, "I'm much better at innovation and growth than I am at dismantling. I felt that I'd done everything that I could do for the company and that a different skill set was necessary." So Phil identified and groomed his replacement, and James Marcum became CEO in late September 2008 when Phil stepped down. Despite a change in leadership, the company later filed for bankruptcy protection.

The process of transforming a company is never without its challenges, and Phil Schoonover has weathered and suffered from his fair share of them. When we asked what he'd learned from the mistakes he'd made along the way, Phil's response related directly to the need to better understand his people, their abilities, and their passions. Like so many of the Transformer archetype, he worked tirelessly to get others engaged around the new direction and overcome fear and resistance. However, he admits to overlooking the requirement to upgrade talent in order to achieve the ambitious goals he had established, even in the face of compelling evidence of the need to do so. "If someone is willing but unable, I will give them the tools to learn," he said. "I'll also give them the benefit of the doubt." The crisis the business was in left little time for developing talent at the top ranks of the company, and the decision to eliminate so many experienced employees at lower levels likely contributed to the company's death spiral.

With uncommon honesty about his own shortcomings, Phil shared one of his more painful lessons. "It's a fair criticism to say that in some instances I've given people in mission-critical positions too much time. I've learned that it is important to put shorter time frames on people stepping up [to the new expectations] and to define better milestones. I've also learned that I have to be humble enough to say 'I don't know how to do this' [if I'm struggling with a part of the transformation] and go out and hire those who do." He also learned that he had to help some other executives leave. "Not everyone is cut out for this kind of work," he said. "When you find that out, you have to deal with it right away because staying too long with a bad decision can be catastrophic."

→ Profile Analysis

Phil Schoonover took on the challenge of repositioning Circuit City for growth at a time in his life and career when proving himself was no longer necessary. He told us life had been good to him and he'd had more opportunities than he had ever imagined. So why would he take on a task to fix Circuit City? Simply because Phil is an executive who thrives on change. "I don't enjoy running things from a status quo perspective," he told us. "I love making new business and fixing things, building high-performing teams, and helping them figure things out." His experience throughout his career has been marked by a willingness to tackle change, from the early years at TOPS and Sony, to his challenges at Circuit City.

Phil's Transformer passion was hardwired and honed in his youth, as he moved seven times during his childhood and "learned how to survive and turn things around." He grew up in Salt Lake City, the son of a Mormon mother and a Catholic father, in a family that became outcasts in the community when his mother converted to Catholicism. Then he watched his mother, with love and compassion, stand up to Mormon family members and rebuild relationships—accomplishing a seemingly impossible task. Perhaps this is the source of his unfailing optimism. "Time and again," he shared, "I proved that nothing is ever as bad as it looks."

Phil demonstrates many strengths of a Transformer. He's excited about change, wants to see the business on a constant path to improvement, and willingly shares his vision for a better way with others. Where he was challenged in the change process at Circuit City was with the vulnerability that Transformers sometimes face:

pushing change too rapidly and unwittingly excluding others in the process. This vulnerability became evident when the initiatives to reduce costs in the business became the focal point of employee time and attention to the detriment of selling and customer service. Phil learned from this experience the importance of engaging employees in creating the vision for the future, rather than merely dictating the destination. He also learned the value of constant examination of priorities when undertaking massive change. "This is an evolving process," he said. "You're really talking about changing [employee] behaviors to get the results you want. We reframed priorities once a quarter, but we were always sure to reinforce that we were a customer service organization." However, this may have been a tougher sell in an organization where experienced employees had been let go.

Phil's Altruist passion is evident in his commitment to corporate citizenship. Under his leadership, Circuit City donated and raised money for Boys and Girls Clubs in every region where they had a retail presence, and Phil served as a trustee in the southeast region. The company also supported the United Way and Habitat for Humanity through the Circuit City Foundation, which through the years has donated over $40 million to charity. During Phil's tenure as CEO, employee volunteerism was promoted, and a commitment to community became an important part of company culture.

His decision to take on the challenges at Circuit City was in part fueled by his desire to create a stronger company for the employees who worked there. Phil was concerned about the impact on their families and future opportunities if the company didn't prosper. "I want to help people," he told us. "That's who I am." The company's demise is no doubt a painful outcome for Phil.

Once he had decided to pursue the transformation of Circuit City, Phil's Altruist passion brought him to a face-off with his teenage son. His son was especially concerned about the toll this challenge would have on their own family. Eventually, Phil helped him understand what was happening in the stores by getting him involved in thinking through what needed to be done to create a stronger platform for success. Together they watched the movie *Pay It Forward*, which Phil said "was an analogy for what we were doing at Circuit City."

Along with the strengths of his Altruist passion, Phil suffered from a vulnerability that made his role in the reshaping of Circuit City so personally challenging. He admits to a tendency to give too much time and support to others who may not have the requisite ability to lead in tumultuous times. To his credit, he recognized this shortcoming and made the necessary changes to the leadership ranks, surrounding himself with other individuals who brought essential strengths to the team, but the decision didn't come soon enough.

Finally, we see the Teacher passion in Phil manifest in his joy of sharing knowledge and mentoring others. He derives great pleasure from helping others learn, and he willingly carved out time in his hectic schedule to provide training to both employee groups and to leaders of the community organizations that Circuit City supported. The leaders playing on his team were also required to take the responsibility for employee development seriously by committing their time to training as well.

With a head, heart, and hands model, Phil worked diligently, but ultimately unsuccessfully, to improve the outlook for the company. While other members of his staff took the lead on parts of this model, "I taught the 'heart' stuff myself," he said with a smile, "because I believe in it." When we asked him to identify the most important element for achieving success with the transformation of Circuit City, Phil told us: "Passion is critical. It's a prerequisite. There is no way you'll be good at this without passion. You can't be Lawrence Welk dancing to MC Hammer. And *this* is Hammer Time!" As we have learned, passion—absent of knowledge and management of its vulnerabilities—can be a fatal flaw. Through this difficult experience, Phil obtained valuable insight that better prepares him to manage the full impact of his passions so that his potential for future success exceeds that achieved earlier in his career.

TEN

The Altruist

LIFE'S MOST PERSISTENT AND URGENT QUESTION IS,
"WHAT ARE YOU DOING FOR OTHERS?"
—MARTIN LUTHER KING, JR.

Profile Overview

Altruists are the humanitarians of the organization. They demonstrate a strong passion for work that benefits the higher good of the organization and society as a whole. Among all the Passion Profile archetypes, the Altruists are the most intensely focused on the impact of work directions and decisions on the larger world. The most talented among this archetype are uniquely capable of holding the objectives of the organization in mind while examining how they can be achieved in a way that is beneficial to all.

The Altruist is likely to be the individual who challenges the organization to develop products or provide services that can be delivered to needy groups or countries at an affordable price. They will work tenaciously in leadership roles or behind the scenes to refine plans, programs, or strategies in a way that recognizes the plight of the less fortunate and designs a way to ameliorate it. This is an archetype that acts as a fierce advocate for others, even when it may not be popular or commonplace to do so.

Experienced Altruists recognize the importance of balancing business goals with the desire to make a positive difference, so that the latter is achieved without compromising the success of the organization. Savvy individuals of this archetype look for business opportunities that allow the organization to do for others as it achieves gain for itself. In this way, the financial framework for supporting societal causes is continually refueled and remains strong.

Altruists build and nurture strong relationships with those that they are trying to assist. They very closely identify with the needs of others and derive great fulfillment from acting as a catalyst to address those needs. While this is a wonderful characteristic, the challenge for some Altruists is in completing the circle of support provided to others. Like a story that they are unable to finish, these Altruists find it difficult to terminate support for a needy group and to allow them to stand on their own. Some individuals of this archetype will struggle with setting boundaries and deadlines that would hold others accountable, so they may be prone to continual giving without making the demands for results that they should.

An important characteristic of the Altruists is the strong sense of self that they derive from their humanitarian activities. Organizations with highly developed Altruists will find that these passionate individuals connect their personal identity and self-worth to the work that they are able to accomplish in service to others. For these individuals, work is truly an extension of who they believe they are at their core—a vehicle for helping society. This in turn is how Altruists will represent their organizations to the world at large. For organizations striving to demonstrate social responsibility, the Altruist is an invaluable asset.

Characteristic Strengths

- Able to look well beyond themselves and their own needs and/or desires
- Passionate about making a positive difference in the world
- Challenge the organization to think about its impact on society
- Promote broad thinking about creative ways to address external needs while achieving internal objectives
- Willing to serve as a catalyst for bringing attention to the needs of those less fortunate, even when this is not a popular position to take

- Deeply committed to their causes and their relationships with others
- Act as a moral compass for the organization

Potential Vulnerabilities

- May have difficulty demanding accountability from others, especially those who are in need or learning
- Can struggle with developing a sense of identity that extends beyond their role in service to others
- If their passion for humanity is not well balanced, may take the sense of self-sacrifice to the level of martyrdom
- May become consumed with a cause to the extent that they are unable to structure an approach that benefits both the needy and the organization
- Sometimes give less of themselves than those closest to them desire (partner, spouse, children) because the context of the Altruists' focus is the larger world

Leading and Managing the Altruists

- Altruists will look to their leaders to provide them with the means to realize the impact of their work, beyond their own department or function. Leaders who consistently make this connection for Altruists wield a powerful lever for securing their ongoing engagement.
- Altruists are driven by high ideals and might occasionally overlook the realities of day-to-day business imperatives. The leaders of this archetype need to help them focus on the task at hand in a way that transforms their high ideals into actionable steps, to facilitate achieving a balance between idealism and realism.
- Remaining open to the Altruists' suggestions for ways in which the organization might connect to its community (both local and global) will foster their continued engagement.
- When companies fail to maintain the highest moral and ethical standards, the Altruists will be the first employees to become disengaged and leave.

- One of the greatest rewards Altruists can receive is seeing a cause that they believe in being supported. Altruists expect more from their organization than financial recognition; they expect to be given roles that allow them to make a tangible contribution to a noble cause.
- When providing feedback to Altruists, their managers should remember that supporting others is the primary motivator for this archetype. Therefore, Altruists will respond well to feedback that demonstrates their management understands and recognizes the positive results they have had with their efforts to support others.

Examples of Roles or Functions in Which This Archetype Thrives

- Executive director of corporate or nonprofit foundation
- Leadership position in organizations that want to demonstrate tangible results in the area of social responsibility
- Civil liberties law (for example, ACLU attorney)
- Employment law
- Nongovernmental aid organizations
- Federal and state youth and family services
- Social worker
- Philanthropist
- Animal rights advocate

Supportive Passion Profile Pairings

- **Builder.** The Builder archetype can assist Altruists in making their high ideals and goals actionable because Builders will orchestrate the achievement of goals in a way that supports the ongoing growth of the business. For example, an Altruist may want to collect donations door to door to raise money to build a school for physically challenged teens. The Builder will organize a national telethon to raise money to build a chain of such schools across the country with plans to grow the program internationally within three years. Builders will expand and enhance the objectives set by Altruists in a way that allows this archetype to achieve more than they imagined possible.

- **Processor.** Processors help to provide monitoring systems to support Altruists so that the results of their work can be tracked and measured. Processors provide a reality check when Altruists want to overextend on support and the data don't indicate that it is possible to do so without harm to the Altruist, the organization, or the recipient of the support. The Processors help curb the Altruists' tendency to give too much of themselves or the goodwill of others.

- **Connector.** Connectors are outstanding partners for Altruists because they help orchestrate relationships with other individuals or organizations that may support their work. Connectors help fill the gap between what Altruists need in order to accomplish their objectives for a cause they believe in and sources that can meet those needs. Because of their broad network, Connectors are able to pull from a variety of sources, which results in an expansion of the attention and focus given to Altruists' work.

Special Care Passion Profile Pairings

- **Healer.** Altruists paired with Healers without another strong archetype to balance the two may result in an abundance of giving to others. The risk for burnout for both archetypes and potentially for those assisting them is high unless the Altruists and the Healers involved have learned to manage the vulnerabilities of their respective archetypes.

Archetype Examples

Mother Teresa of Calcutta.   Missionary, humanitarian, Roman Catholic nun

Dr. Martin Luther King, Jr.   Clergyman, activist, leader of the civil rights movement

Marian Wright Edelman.   Founder and president of the Children's
Defense Fund

 ## The Altruist's Story: John Wood

Primary profile. *Altruist*
Secondary profiles.   *Builder, Connector*

John Wood is the founder and CEO of Room to Read, a nonprofit
organization dedicated to building libraries and schools in some
of the most impoverished areas of Asia and Africa. Under his leadership, the organization establishes 2,000 libraries per year, with a goal
of 2,500 per year by 2010. Compare its results to those of Wood's hero,
Andrew Carnegie, who completed just 2,500 libraries in his *lifetime,*
and one can't help but be impressed by Room to Read's results.

The path to philanthropy was anything but traditional for John.
Back in the late 1990s, he was living the good life. As a single, hand-
some, thirty-something executive for Microsoft, John had landed
coveted overseas assignments in Australia and China. He had an
apartment overlooking Sydney's famous harbor, a luxury car with a
personal driver, and a lifestyle in the high-rent district of the city. He
was running fast and hard, growing the business for an industry giant in the "invent it today or die tomorrow" culture of the technology
world. John was at the top of his game, making more money than he
had ever dreamed possible, and as an international markets specialist, he traveled in style to places around the globe. High pressure and
stress were part of his daily diet, but John functioned with the mantra
"You can sleep when you are dead and buried." In his world, vacations
were a luxury that would be reserved for retirement.

Over time, John's corporate ninja lifestyle caught up with him. By
the age of 34, he began to feel uneasy. Seven years of intercontinental travel, midnight conference calls, and high-stakes meetings with
Bill Gates and Steve Ballmer in countries critical to Microsoft's future
left him weary, disconnected from family and friends, and wondering

if his life should count for more. While relaxing on a tropical beach might have been a choice for many fatigued executives, John chose a strenuous 18-day, 200-mile trek in the Himalayas, with a fully loaded backpack, to unwind from his busy lifestyle—the corporate warrior in him was not quite ready to give up the fight.

It was a choice that changed his life.

Looking for an opportunity to reassess his future, John went to Nepal and "sat by a river to contemplate life." John believes that being in nature in a remote environment while writing in his journal allows him to access a part of his brain that is unavailable to him during the hectic pace of his daily workday.

On this trip, a chance meeting over a dusty bottle of beer in an outdoor café brought him face-to-face with the serious impact of poverty on the education of children in the region. He struck up a conversation with a Nepali man at a neighboring table and learned that the country's illiteracy rate was 70 percent, and like its mountains, it was among the highest in the world. Curious to learn more about the plight of children in the country, John joined the man the next day on a hike to a school in a remote village. There he met dedicated educators in a small classroom crammed with 70 students, all of whom politely bid him a "good morning," spoken in perfect English. The headmaster invited John on a tour of the school, which ended in a sparsely stocked library. It was a tidy room with an out-of-date map on the wall, but it had no books except for a few dog-eared novels and texts inappropriate for children, left behind by tourists. There were 450 kids in a school with no books! As a passionate reader since childhood, John decided at that moment that he could make a difference. It was a pivotal decision that eventually led him far from his executive lifestyle.

Over the years that he was based in Australia and then in China, John had increasingly begun to question the direction his life was taking, and he had also begun to doubt how his work was helping him to shape a life of meaning. "I felt like I was devoting all of my waking hours to making people richer," he shared. The trip to Nepal to "relax" only increased his internal unrest, so much so that within 12 months of his visit to the school, John realized his commitment to Microsoft was fading. The chance encounter with Nepali children had helped him find what his job in a multi-billion-dollar company could not: his purpose, which John says is "to figure out how to take my good fortune in life—a great education, a great family, and making lots of money at a young age—and use that good fortune to make a difference in the world."

When trying to work within Microsoft to promote activities that would support needy communities, John often encountered resistance. He felt the company had a great platform for changing the world but that Microsoft was missing opportunities to make a positive difference. Although Bill Gates has supported a host of causes through his foundation and has more recently urged companies to create businesses that focus on building products and services for the poor, this philosophy had not taken hold in the company at that time.[1]

When John questioned Steve Ballmer about Microsoft's position on a community giving project that he had proposed, Ballmer indicated that it was Microsoft's job to create shareholder value. If the shareholders wanted to then donate their earnings to societal causes, that was their decision. "I respected Steve Ballmer for giving us clarity," John told us. "The great thing about Steve is that you always get a straight answer from him. It helped me to know that Microsoft wasn't the right place for me because it wasn't going to provide me with the opportunity to live my purpose." So, amid the dismay and shock of his boss and colleagues, John resigned from his position as director of business development for the Greater China region, and he closed the chapter on his life at Microsoft.

The challenge of founding Room to Read was not easy. As with any start-up organization, finding donors was a critical aspect of success. One might think that an executive with connections like John's would have no problem networking his way to the money required to make the idea of Room to Read a reality. But having such connections does not always mean success in fund-raising for a new nonprofit. John learned that individuals that he thought were supportive friends disappeared when the requests for money began. However, some friends at Microsoft did try to help out by booking the main theater for a presentation that John was scheduled to deliver, in hopes of generating interest and support for his project. To his great disappointment, only eight people showed up. So along with making the monumental decision to leave a comfortable corporate job, John also faced the unpleasant truth about the individuals he thought would be in his corner.

Later in the process of building the organization, John received a jarring introduction to the importance of courage on his journey to materializing his dreams. "People thought I was crazy or going through a midlife crisis," he shared. "We didn't have an endowment. I didn't have $50 million in the bank; I had $2 million. So in order to go big, I had to be fund-raising from Day 1. In leaving a prominent corporate position, I had to accept a loss in my social status, which in itself wasn't a big deal. I wasn't flying in first class anymore; I was in the back of the plane. But then the stock market melted down in 2000, and in our second year as an organization, September 11 struck, and the markets plunged further. I watched the money disappear that I thought I had as a foundation. I think if I had known all of this when I started, I would never have done it." Although his parents would describe him as the kind of kid who would give you the shirt off his back, John was in for a bigger uphill battle than he expected.

Despite these early challenges, his determination paid off. John could count on the support of his family and close friends, but he was also able to attract the interest of some venture capitalists who became early donors. The Draper Richards Foundation, along with Sequoia Capital Founder, Don Valentine, his wife, Rachel, and their daughter, Hilary, supported the business model that John had conceived, and they believed in him personally, which was a big boost to his confidence at a time when it was sorely needed. The networking and hard work paid off so well that about 90 percent of the current donors to Room to Read are not individuals that John knew when he started the nonprofit.

His ability to engage others in his dream has allowed John to build a staff that works tirelessly to define and achieve the organization's objectives. "I look for people who are action-oriented optimists," he says. "When people are passionate, they'll do anything; they'll run through walls for the business, if that's what it takes to deliver educational opportunities to kids."

That passion is paying off. Room to Read is making a difference in the education of children in some of the world's neediest countries. Over 2 million students have access to the schools and libraries Room to Read is creating. The organization is now reaching children in Cambodia, India, Laos, Nepal, Sri Lanka, South Africa, Vietnam, and Zambia. It is providing scholarships to girls in developing countries, allowing many to attend school for the first time. It has established over 7,000 libraries, and the numbers just keep growing. John credits the thousands of volunteers working in 37 cities around the world for Room to Read's success. Collectively, they have raised over $20 million in the last four years. "I'm the leader of this movement, but I couldn't do anything without the people who have chosen to be involved," said John.

Given this track record, we asked John about his ultimate objective for the organization. What he told us was both characteristically courageous and daunting. "When I first started this, I did research to find the Andrew Carnegie of the developing world," he said. "There wasn't one—nothing on a massive scale. So I decided, I guess it's me and the talented team that I can attract. Room to Read will be the Carnegie of the developing world. I've set that as our vision. And I believe that bold goals attract bold people." As head of an organization dedicated to universal education, John Wood is an entrepreneur with a great big heart.

➡ Profile Analysis

To most executives tucked safely away in a plum corporate job, John Wood is either courageous or crazy. He is an accomplished businessman in his own right, but he is also an entrepreneur with a plan to change the world. The Altruist in John does not allow him to stand silently by while so many of the world's impoverished children succumb to a fate born of illiteracy—a future of limited hope and dwindling opportunity.

During his tenure at Microsoft, John challenged the company to think about its impact on society. Like many of his passion archetype, he acted as one of the organization's moral compasses when it came to Microsoft's ability to make a difference in the communities it served. It gradually became apparent to John that the company's vision of its community responsibility in the areas in which he had an interest did not match his view of the company's potential to make a difference; he knew it was time to leave and pursue his own path.

While his Altruist passion drove him to take personal responsibility for making a difference for children, it was the strengths of that passion that allowed the level of his success to be tempered only by the size of his dreams. Room to Read under John's leadership has been a remarkable success and a major force in changing the plight of children around the world.

The unique Passion Archetype Cluster of Altruist/Builder/Connector proved a powerful combination that allowed John to weather the early years of building the organization, especially the transition period following the events surrounding the attacks on September 11, 2001. Someone with an Altruist passion who lacked the added strengths of the Builder and Connector passions might have succumbed to the discouragement, fear, and disappointment that John no doubt felt during those early days. It was the Builder passion coupled with the Altruist in John that prompted him to pull himself up by his bootstraps and set stretch goals for fund-raising, library and school construction, and outreach to needy countries. His plans were not to send volunteers door to door to collect spare change from their neighbors. Instead, he wanted to build an organization that could create a sustained difference in the access to learning for children in the developing world. To do that, he would need money . . . and lots of it.

His Connector passion became an important ally in establishing funding for Room to Read, as John discovered that a fast-lane life in the corporate world did not necessarily translate to a wellspring of access to high-end donors for a fledgling NGO. The passion for reaching out to others, sharing the potential of Room to Read, and getting donors and thousands of volunteers excited about playing a part in changing children's lives for the better helped John's lofty dreams reach fruition. He was persistent in telling his story, engaging potential contributors, identifying talent to execute the organization's plans, and setting bold goals for the future. In John's opinion, thinking big will attract those who want to achieve great things. And in a world where there are so many immense problems to be solved, incremental thinking is just not enough.

ELEVEN

The Healer

I AM A HUMAN BEING, SO THERE IS NOTHING HUMAN
THAT I DO NOT FEEL TO BE OF MY CONCERN.
—TERENCE (190–159 BC)

Profile Overview

Healers are a gift to any organization. While many appear in traditional forms such as physicians, nurses, therapists, or other medical practitioners, Healers may also be organizational leaders, first-line supervisors, or the coworkers on the floor of the manufacturing plant. This archetype appears in many forms beyond those classically associated with treating disease. Regardless of organizational level, Healers carry with them a passion for creating peace where there is turmoil, applying salve to open wounds, and mending broken relationships or broken spirits.

An archetype that is particularly passionate about sinking to the root cause of an issue, Healers will use both their intellect and informed intuition to do so. This allows Healers to accurately diagnose situations and determine whether the behaviors or manifestations they are observing are actually driven by internal factors or whether they are influenced by external circumstance. As excellent observers of others and of what is going on around them, Healers deeply examine the underlying causes of dissention, pain, or discomfort in a way that exceeds what other archetypes are able to understand. They demonstrate a unique willingness to venture into an unhealthy situation to offer assistance, when most other people would not.

Healers are invaluable in the effort to repair dysfunctional organizations or in mediating differences between coworkers. With an unusual level of patience and understanding, they create a peaceful, safe space into which others may enter to share their concerns and burdens. This archetype is especially valuable when implementing mergers and acquisitions, joint ventures, or other large-scale organizational changes in which jobs or routines may be disrupted in ways that result in chaos or fear among employees. Healers are also a critical archetype to assign to positions where the aftermath of a previous leader has left the organization demoralized, as they are uniquely able to help others to move past their pain and focus on a more positive future. The Healers' ultimate objective is to examine the full spectrum of the individual, the organization, or the situation at hand in order to discover how to nourish the whole so that health is restored.

Characteristic Strengths

- High degree of emotional intelligence and empathy
- Outstanding ability to identify the root source of pain or dysfunction
- Able to help others transform pain into a healing process
- Embrace differences easily and value others
- Able to create positive shifts in the energy of a group
- Excellent observers of others and have the ability to identify needs
- Strong desire to connect to others in meaningful ways
- Highly unselfish

Potential Vulnerabilities

- May be overly generous with time
- Can suffer from self-neglect
- May become overly burdened with others' problems
- At times may create situations in which others become overly dependent
- Can intensely identify with another's pain and be negatively impacted by it

- May multitask to the point of exhaustion
- Work is often below the radar so all contributions may not be recognized, leaving Healers feeling undervalued and resentful

Leading and Managing the Healers

- Healers are so often sought out by others for assistance that what they are managing can rapidly increase beyond that which has been assigned to them. Attention needs to be paid to how much they take on.
- Healers will gravitate toward healing even if it is not a specific component of their organizational role. Assignments and workloads will need to be structured with this fact in mind.
- Healers are a go-to archetype when the organization is facing a crisis.
- Healers can be counted on to help repair strained relationships among team members, but leaders should not abdicate their own responsibilities for managing team dynamics.
- Healers are so often engaged in helping others that they rarely focus enough on their own needs. The leader of individuals of this archetype should provide them with opportunities to "recharge."
- It's important for the leader to occasionally be a sounding board and allow the Healers to unload all that they are burdened with. In essence, the leader must perform the role for Healers that Healers perform for so many others.
- When things appear to be working smoothly, the unobservant leader may not recognize the fine hand of the Healer in the background orchestrating the desired outcomes. It is, therefore, important for the leader of this archetype to remain vigilant about recognizing the Healer's contribution so that the Healer does not feel undervalued.

Examples of Roles or Functions in Which This Archetype Thrives

- Positions in organization development and training
- Customer service representative

- Employee relations specialist
- Supplier relationship management positions
- Clinical medicine
- Allied health professions
- Executive coaching
- Mergers and acquisitions teams
- Joint venture leadership positions
- Large-scale change management projects

Supportive Passion Profile Pairings

- **Connector.**   This archetype is a valuable ally to Healers, especially when they need access to others in the organization who might be counted on to provide solutions for a problem situation that the Healers are helping to manage.
- **Teacher.**   Healers will reach out to Teachers when they are assisting those in the organization who may be struggling in their role or are in need of mentoring. Teachers support Healers in alleviating others' pain by providing developmental guidance where it is needed.
- **Transformer.**   Healers and Transformers provide vital support to one another during times of change, which invariably impacts the culture and morale of the organization and may affect relationships with customers and suppliers. Healers can serve as barometers for the pain and fear that others are experiencing within the organization or externally, and they can assist Transformers with helping them to navigate through change.

Special Care Passion Profile Pairings

- **Altruist.**   The pairing of Healers with Altruists without another strong archetype to balance the two may result in an abundance of giving to others. The risk for burnout for both archetypes and for those assisting them is high, so it is important that the Altruist and the Healer involved recognize and learn to manage the vulnerabilities of their respective archetypes.

Archetype Examples

Andrew Weil, M.D.　　Author, physician, leading proponent of integrative medicine

Deepak Chopra, M.D.　　Author, physician, mind-body medicine expert

 The Healer's Story: Dr. Ben Carson

Primary profile. *Healer*

Secondary profiles. *Conceiver, Altruist*

Ben Carson grew up in inner city Detroit, where many young black youth in his neighborhood turned to crime and drugs to numb the dismal reality of the limited opportunities available to them. Ben and his brother, Curtis, might have suffered the same fate had it not been for the strength and determination of their mother and the solid religious underpinning with which she raised her children. Sonya Carson, a woman who was unable to read and had only a third-grade education, managed to raise her boys into responsible men, one of whom became an engineer and the other a world-renowned pediatric neurosurgeon.

Since the age of 33, Ben Carson has been the director of pediatric neurosurgery at Johns Hopkins Medical Institutions, where he makes a difference in the lives of sick children and their families every day. But the journey to the pinnacle of success he currently enjoys was not an easy path for Ben. Although he had decided when he was a young boy that he wanted to be a physician (after hearing stories in church about missionary doctors), Ben was not a good student in his early years, and he suffered from a temper that threatened to land him in jail. Despite the challenges of poverty and personality, Ben turned his grades around, learned to manage his temper, and worked his way into a full scholarship at Yale. He later graduated from the University of Michigan Medical School.

Now a gentle, soft-spoken father of three, this gifted physician has performed some of the most complicated surgical procedures of anyone in his field. The case that earned Ben international acclaim was the successful separation of the seven-month-old Binder twins, who were conjoined at the head, a condition that occurs only once in every 2 to 2.5 million births. Healer that he is, Ben couldn't pass up the opportunity to try to help the boys and their parents, even though the odds for their survival were limited. "I went into pediatric neurosurgery because I like to get a good return on my investment," Ben told us with a smile. "Giving someone 60 or more years of a quality life is a fantastic thing to do. It doesn't have to be the most newsworthy case for me to want to make a difference."

Like many of his archetype, Ben carries a great sense of responsibility for others. Early on in his medical career, he remembers "walking through the wards and seeing all of these high-powered folks who were patients dying of horrible diseases. I learned then that I was dealing with the most important thing that a person has: his or her life." His choice to express his passion through his role as a surgeon is a choice that Ben made based on an assessment of his talents. What keeps him there is the opportunity to ease others' pain and suffering. "I don't particularly like surgery, . . . at least not cutting people open and seeing blood," he admitted. "I know my talents include being able to think in three dimensions, having good hand-eye coordination, being meticulous, and being able to solve problems. But it's my desire to give people longevity and a quality of life that drives me."

One of the most challenging aspects of Ben's passion is dealing with the demands he places on himself. "I always feel that I could be doing more and doing better, . . . figuring out how I could be preventing things from going wrong," he told us. "I feel burdened by a sense of inadequacy sometimes, and I never feel that I have done my best, especially if things don't turn out perfectly." The mammoth sense of responsibility he carries is coupled with a tendency to devote too much of himself to his patients. He spent years working nearly seven days a week, before hiring additional neurosurgeons to the staff. Having done so, Ben can now "pull back a bit," but he admits to still giving away too much. While his family continues to believe that he works too hard, Ben counters with his own assessment of the situation: "I always feel that to those to whom much is given, much is expected," he said. "There is just so much that has to be done." He credits his faith with helping him manage well in a stressful profession, acknowledging his belief that the outcome of his work is ultimately all in God's hands. But Ben insists that coping would be far more difficult if he didn't give each surgery his fullest effort and the patient died as a result. "That would really plague me," he said.

In recent years, Ben's connection to his patients has grown even deeper because of a health crisis of his own. He was diagnosed with prostate cancer, and an MRI showed lesions up and down his spine. Certain he was facing a death sentence, Ben began to take stock of his life. "I had always wondered how I would face death," he candidly stated. "I went home that day, took a walk around our property, and started noticing the life around me even more. I realized then that it didn't bother me that I was going to die. I felt I'd go to a better place. The worst thing for me was disappointing others—my family and my patients."

As fate would have it, Ben's cancer was not responsible for the lesions on his spine, and the tumor on his prostate was successfully removed. He has many healthy years ahead of him, and he credits three important lessons to this experience:

1. *It's difficult to reverse your role as a Healer. "I had to keep telling myself you are the patient," he said.*
2. *Ben's own brush with death has helped him to better convey a sense of peace to patients who are going to die. He believes it is comforting to others that he now understands their experience from a firsthand perspective.*
3. *Since everyone at the hospital went out of their way to help Ben through the crisis, he has no doubt that he received special care. This experience prompted Ben to tell his staff, "We have one standard of care for everyone: excellence. Everyone is special. When children are sick, their parents are not rational—they're worried. They need us to be rational and kind."*

Ben Carson is unusually humble for a man with his accomplishments, and he has managed to avoid the stereotypical demeanor of the arrogant surgeon. He has won numerous honorary degrees and awards for his work—most recently the National Medal of Freedom, which is the highest civilian honor that can be bestowed upon an American. Upon receiving this most prestigious recognition, Ben put it all in perspective for the audience at the White House: "Whether we get medals or special recognition is really not that important. What's really important is that you do the very best that you can, that you take personal responsibility . . . not only in your own life but in those who are in your sphere of influence."

Since the late 1980s, Ben has received hundreds of thousands of letters from patients, their families, and total strangers about the positive effect he's had on their lives. Those letters helped him to understand that he is a Healer with a platform to make a difference in the world. It's a responsibility that Ben believes extends well beyond the surgical suite. He has used this platform to become an international speaker and author with a powerful, inspiring message about nurturing our youth to develop them into great future leaders. Over the last two decades he has become increasingly concerned with children's education and alarmed by the growing attrition rates in schools and the country's lagging academic performance compared to other nations. With an ongoing commitment to improving the quality of life for others, he and his wife, Candy, founded the Carson Scholars Fund to recognize and reward students who strive for academic excellence. To date, the program has awarded over 3,400 scholarships to children in 26 states for attendance at four-year colleges and universities.

Ben has serious concerns about another important issue getting prominent media attention today: the health-care crisis in America. As a physician, he performs complex, expensive procedures that would challenge the insurance and savings of any family. But what of the patients who do not have insurance but have a serious medical condition? In the past, Ben was able to write off expenses if the family couldn't afford a needed procedure, but with skyrocketing health-care costs, that is no longer possible.

Denying patients treatment because they can't afford the therapy isn't an option in Ben's opinion, so he has taken a courageous and creative approach to address the problem. With the help of attorney Ron Shapiro and colleague Dr. Cliff Solomon, he started a nonprofit fund known as "Angels of the OR" to provide the critical surgery that needy patients can't afford. His idea is to create an endowment fund of such significant size that the medical expenses of the neediest can be paid from the interest alone. Angels of the OR is an experiment that might just provide some long-sought solutions to the health-care crisis in America. In Ben's opinion, setting aside just 10 percent of the total national dollars spent on health care over the next 10 to 15 years could create a national endowment that would make universal health care possible. A lofty goal, no doubt, but one that a kid who grew up in the slums of Detroit and became a gifted surgeon and Healer believes is possible to achieve.

→ Profile Analysis

Ben Carson demonstrates many of the finest characteristics of a Healer, as well as some of the vulnerabilities of this archetype. Most notable is his incredible compassion for his patients and their families. He devotes a great deal of time and effort to helping them understand the patients' illnesses and the options available to treat their conditions, but he also assists them in transitioning through the fear and panic that sets in when a child becomes seriously ill. Ben connects with his patients' pain and fear and meets it head on—a characteristic response that he has demonstrated throughout his career. A personal brush with cancer has only enhanced his qualities as a Healer because it has created in Ben a closer connection to the patients' own experiences.

Sitting in his presence during the interview, we could not help but be struck by the sense of calm and kindness that marks his demeanor. Like many Healers, Ben is able to create a field of serenity around him, despite the stress and fatigue that he must experience in a role in which life and death decisions are made on a daily basis. It is that very environment that he strives to create for his patients by encouraging his staff to be kind and centered, even when the parents of sick children are not able to be the same.

Like many Healers, Ben struggles with limiting how much of himself he gives away to others. His strong level of empathy and desire to take responsibility for patients' well-being results in Ben's spending a great deal of time with them, . . . perhaps more than he should. In shouldering an excessive level of responsibility for the welfare of his patients, Ben has found himself with an additional burden, bearing an unjustified sense of inadequacy about his work. Many Healers grapple with establishing the internal boundaries that will allow them to define the limits of their responsibility for another's well-being. If they are especially capable like Ben, the challenge is even more difficult because this archetype views the ability to heal as indistinguishable from the responsibility to do so.

Peppered throughout his story are also signs of the Conceiver and Altruist in Ben Carson. Evidence of his Altruist passion can be seen in his decision to address the problems of education and health care in America by establishing scholarship and endowment funds to serve the neediest students and patients. It is not enough to acknowledge the need; his passion compels him to address it actively and tangibly.

Ben recognizes his ability to think three dimensionally, which is a characteristic trait of Conceivers who may actually think in even more than three. He is also able to hold enormous volumes of complex information in mind, sift through that which is most relevant, and navigate to reach appropriate solutions. It's hard to imagine a more challenging environment, fraught with more potential landmines and opportunities for disaster, than performing surgery on the human brain. Yet this is the environment in which Ben works and in which he makes innumerable decisions during any one procedure. He must simultaneously grasp the complexities of the patient's condition and operate on an extremely delicate part of the body. And he must possess a deep understanding about the ramifications of every move he makes, all the while trying to repair a damaged segment of the organ. With procedures that can take almost 24 hours to complete in the most difficult cases, Ben's work requires that he exercise not only his Healer and Conceiver passions but his stamina as well.

TWELVE

The Teacher

ALL NEW KNOWLEDGE GLADDENS [THE TEACHER] ONLY
TO THE EXTENT THAT HE CAN TEACH IT.
—FRIEDRICH NIETZSCHE

Profile Overview

Teachers are integral contributors to the lineage of organizational knowledge. They help to create the foundation of institutional wisdom—the single greatest organizational asset as yet unaccounted for on the balance sheet. Through a strong passion for sharing and assimilating knowledge, teachers support the development and learning of others. By doing so, Teachers increase their own knowledge and understanding, thereby continually fueling and nurturing the Knowledge Cycle of the organization.

Many individuals in this Passion Profile archetype gravitate toward teaching early in their careers, although not all of them choose traditional teaching roles within the organization. Regardless of position, the passion for teaching will manifest strongly for those of this archetype, and their value will quickly be recognized by others who are longing to learn or who are burdened with unresolved challenges that require new understanding. Teachers, always passionate about new information and new ways of viewing the world around them, happily provide food to the hungry minds that they encounter.

Teachers carry with them a strong sense of responsibility for the role that they play in the transfer and assimilation of knowledge. They enter into the teaching relationship with reverence and respect for the

135

learner, fully cognizant of the fact that fertile minds are the organization's most precious resource. Ultimately the Teacher's focus is to both pass on wisdom and develop the learner's character.

Many Teachers demonstrate a degree of generosity with their knowledge that is beyond the norm. They readily share all that they have learned, requiring in return only openness to new information or ways of thinking. This distinct archetypal quality is in stark contrast to the jealous guarding of knowledge (and the power associated with it) that is characteristic of some organizational cultures. For Teachers, the passion for growing the body of knowledge is an underlying driver in much of what they do. As a result, they are particularly impacted when they perceive that knowledge is hoarded or inefficiently disseminated rather than freely shared.

With a strong desire to establish long-lasting interaction with the student, be it someone they are teaching in a traditional fashion or a work colleague that they may be mentoring, Teachers build relationships on a foundation of mutual respect. They are pleased to be viewed as someone who has something to teach, and they strive to help others see that they are worthy of being taught. In the best of situations, this is a relationship of equals in which the Teacher views the student as an intellectual companion on the journey to developing new knowledge or a deeper understanding of previously held information. In the journey of equals, it does not matter that the Teacher may hold more knowledge about a subject area than the student. The joy in the process for the Teacher is the student's accomplishment in learning.

Teachers are particularly adept at translating information in a variety of ways, so that the learner can understand new or complex concepts with ease. They quickly determine creative ways to communicate knowledge so that the learner can readily access it. Some Teachers are visual translators of knowledge, drawing pictures (actual or intellectual) for the student. Einstein, for example, was well known for his "thought experiments," which he used to describe complex theoretical physics concepts to his students and fellow scientists as well as to formulate his groundbreaking theories. Others of this archetype teach through the senses, helping their students to learn through visual, auditory, or kinesthetic routes.

The most passionate Teachers thrive in the question as much as the answer, and they enjoy exchanging knowledge through discussion and debate, where all involved in the process might discover new ways of looking at things. Therefore, truth is a highly prized commodity to Teachers, and it is the underpinning of their work with others. They willingly devote whatever time is necessary to discovering true insights into intellectual challenges, and they will tenaciously research to discern fact from fiction. They do all of this because they value the student and they value knowledge, and they want to pass on only high-quality learning. This is true of individuals manifesting the Teacher archetype in the corporate environment or in the traditional classroom setting.

Teachers are also passionate learners because acquiring new information and deeper understanding is at the heart of this archetype. Many show interest in a wide array of subjects, although some Teachers may choose to specialize in a particular body of knowledge. In any case, the Teachers' thirst for learning is never abated, which means that they consistently bring an energy and enthusiasm to their work provided there is new knowledge to be acquired. Individuals with this Passion Profile who are placed in the right job describe their experience as one in which they do not feel they are going to work each day; rather, they feel they are going out to share what they love to do . . . going to "school."

Characteristic Strengths

- Strong sense of commitment and connection to the learner
- Passion for growing a body of knowledge in their preferred subject area
- Passion for developing others
- Ability to translate information in a variety of ways that enhance learning

- Openness to discussion and debate
- Are themselves passionate learners
- Committed to sharing the truth in their area of expertise

Potential Vulnerabilities

- May overextend themselves in an effort to share knowledge
- Can take on too much responsibility for others' learning success
- May not recognize and acknowledge their own past accomplishments, especially if they experience failure with helping a learner
- May view others' lack of interest in their area of expertise as a sign of disrespect
- Because they are absorbed with a particular subject, may lose sight of day-to-day responsibilities
- Can be viewed as pontificating when trying to share *all* that they know about a subject
- When devoting time to an enthusiastic learner, can be perceived as showing favoritism

Leading and Managing the Teachers

- Teachers often view their leader as their teacher.
- They thrive on exchange and dialogue in environments in which ongoing learning is valued. Leaders or managers of Teachers must value and stimulate the high-quality thinking within the organization that keeps the Teachers engaged.
- Teachers enjoy leaders who can appreciate another's intellect without allowing their own ego to interfere and who give them assignments designed to stimulate thinking and foster continued learning.
- Teachers thrive on intimacy in a relationship with a learner. They favor quality of relationships over web building. Be cautious to not overload the Teachers with more people to mentor than they can reasonably handle.

- Teachers can easily become absorbed in exploring a topic of interest and set aside other work to do so. This archetype works best when timelines are established for accomplishing objectives.
- They need to be provided enough freedom for experimentation and exploring new ideas. Establishing a culture in which taking risks is valued serves as an important source of excitement for this archetype.
- When assessing the performance of Teachers, it is critical for the leaders of this archetype to demonstrate that they are genuinely interested in the growth and development of the Teachers, or the Teachers are likely to disengage from the relationship.

Examples of Roles or Functions in Which This Archetype Thrives

- Director of training and development
- Organization development specialist
- Director of consumer education
- Vice president of medical education
- Director of employee development
- Vice president of talent management
- Consumer education specialist
- Traditional academic roles
- Any leadership position in which the development of less experienced employees is a key objective

Supportive Passion Profile Pairings

- **Conceiver.** Conceivers thrive in creating new knowledge, which is a natural complement to Teachers, who thrive on sharing knowledge and learning.
- **Processor.** Processors capably analyze information and are able to take complex data and dissect it in ways that help others understand it. They provide a useful service to Teachers, who can then share the information with others.

- **Discoverer.** With a desire to pursue the truth and explore the unknown, Discoverers support the Teachers' commitment to sharing high-quality information backed by evidence to support it.

Special Care Passion Profile Pairings

- **Transformer.** Change processes frequently cause a disruption in the flow of knowledge and assimilation of information as rapid adjustments to the way work gets accomplished are implemented. This may frustrate or alienate the Teachers or leave them feeling unneeded or undervalued.
- **Builder.** Often fast-paced in their desire to accomplish goals, Builders have in their minds a limited amount of time to review knowledge for the sake of the intellectual exercise alone. As such, they may be at odds with Teachers, who want to extensively share their knowledge, which is time-consuming. This situation, coupled with the Builders' sometimes brusque, business-focused manner may leave the Teachers feeling disrespected.

Archetype Examples

Barbara Morgan.   Teacher/astronaut who flew on the space shuttle *Endeavor* and conducted science experiments from space, which were shared by video with schoolchildren

Michael Geisen.   Middle school science teacher, 2008 National Teacher of the Year

 The Teacher's Story: Ysaye Barnwell, Ph.D.

Primary profile.   *Teacher*
Secondary profiles.   *Creator, Processor*

In the late 1930s, the three square miles that comprise Harlem was home to 175,000 African Americans who had migrated from the South for greater opportunity. This period in Manhattan's history marked the Harlem Renaissance, a time of intellectual and cultural blossoming. In an explosion of literature, music, and art, a revolutionary form of group expression and self-determination redefined African Americans in this country. One cannot help but imagine the luminaries of that time who made the Harlem Renaissance such an important historical period: writers W. E. B. DuBois and Langston Hughes; poet Zora Neale Hurston; jazz greats Duke Ellington and Cab Calloway performing at the Cotton Club; and actress Josephine Baker on stage. This was the world inhabited by Irving and Marcella, the parents of singer Ysaye Barnwell.

Some 16 years following this flowering in African American culture, Ysaye came into the world, born to a mother who was a registered nurse and a father who was an accomplished musician/teacher. These educated African American parents were dedicated to Ysaye's growth and development.

She received her musical training at her father's knee, which prepared Ysaye for her current position as executive director and singing member of Sweet Honey in the Rock, a popular African American women's a cappella group. Although Irving Barnwell founded the Coleridge Taylor String Quartet (perhaps the greatest quartet the race has known) and played in Dean Dixon's orchestra and the orchestra of *Shuffle Along* (written by legendary ragtime pianist, Eubie Blake and lyricist Noble Sissle), he focused Ysaye's education strictly on the classics, from the time that she was age two.

"When I was about 12, my father lost his sight because of glaucoma," she shared. "I had been watching him teach piano and violin all my life, so I was able to assist him with teaching his students." That experience, coupled with making friends with a hearing impaired girl from Haiti and a chance opportunity to see *The Miracle Worker* (the story of Anne Sullivan's struggle to teach blind and deaf Helen Keller how to speak), triggered Ysaye's interest in teaching. "I was fascinated with the idea that you could teach folks who couldn't hear how to talk," she told us.

Years later, Ysaye studied speech pathology and became interested in related areas such as brain injury, cleft palate, and stuttering, and she eventually went on to earn both a bachelor's and a master's degree in speech pathology and a Ph.D. in craniofacial studies. She found herself among a small number of people of color pursuing a degree in that field.

"When I moved into my dorm at college [in upstate New York], many of the students had never even been close to a black person. So I created a library of books about high-quality African Americans, which helped those who were interested better understand our culture." In a school where Ysaye was one of only seven blacks, educating fellow students was an uphill battle.

The assassination of Dr. Martin Luther King, Jr., and the racial discord that followed marked a pivotal moment in her life. Close to graduating, Ysaye decided that she wanted to teach in a black environment, so she later accepted a job offer at Howard University in Washington, D.C., a town still smoldering from the racial riots of the 1960s. These events in Ysaye's early years sparked a lifelong interest in black history and a desire to help others understand African American culture.

After 12 years at Howard, Ysaye was unsuccessful in obtaining tenure, even after promotion to full professor, and she was in search of other professional opportunities. At that time a chance visit to a local church changed the course of the rest of her life. "I ended up joining a choir at a Unitarian church," she remembered. "For that choir, you really had to read music because they performed very complicated pieces. I decided to start a choir that didn't require participants to read music, and some time later I convinced the minister to offer a service on disabilities." Not only did Ysaye sing her first solo in church on that Sunday, she also signed the lyrics. As fate would have it, in the congregation that eventful day was Dr. Bernice Johnson Reagon, founder of Sweet Honey, a group growing in popularity and in search of new members.

Ysaye successfully auditioned for the group, and during her first year as a member earned a postdoctoral master's degree in public health while performing with them. Her passion for knowledge had not subsided. "Five years later, I was sitting in a financial institution, trying to get loan approval to buy a condo," she recalled. "That's when I realized that my work with Sweet Honey was actually how I was

paying my bills. I had made it as a musician!" Ysaye also realized that
what she wanted to accomplish as a teacher was actually being realized through her work as a performer. "Sweet Honey became a larger
platform for who I am and what I do. I haven't really stopped teaching," she said. "Three years after joining the group, I started doing
workshops on Building a Vocal Community," which Ysaye conducts
at various venues around the world.

Through her workshops, Ysaye has created a powerful process
that gets even nonmusical types singing. We've witnessed her work in
local communities where she'll enter a room full of willing (and unwilling) amateurs and transform the group into a choir of voices that
rivals those heard at the National Cathedral.

Now, a word should be said about her gifted voice. Ysaye has an
incredible range! She can sing every part in the choir from bass to first
soprano, breaking the song down into discreet pieces. It's this gift that
supports her work with building vocal communities—she can easily
teach each part by example, making it simple for even amateurs to
learn their portion of a song and experience joy while performing it.

The objective of Ysaye's work extends beyond the beauty of the
music; it's driven by high ideals. "I get folks singing, and through
that process, they're learning about the history and values of African
Americans," she shared. "Through song they learn about the African
American worldview and how that has shaped our music and the way
we work in the world." Ysaye's lesson is a powerful one of tolerance,
acceptance, and love.

A prolific writer and composer, she has created many of the contemporary pieces for the Grammy winning ensemble Sweet Honey in
the Rock. Her message has been translated into illustrated children's
books, as well as music for dance, choral, and film productions. In
1998, she appeared in Oprah Winfrey's movie *Beloved*, along with
other members of Sweet Honey.

In the future years of her career, Ysaye hopes to pass on her knowledge. She is often sought out by others for advice, and she has been
a mentor to five people over the last several years, despite a demanding travel and performance schedule that takes her around the globe.

While she might like to coach even more young people, each performance she gives is really an act of mentoring and teaching, helping her audience to embrace differences and value the diversity that comprises our world. Perhaps Ysaye's message is best summed up in the lyrics of a song she wrote in 1993 that is still relevant today:

We Are . . .

For each child that's born
a morning star rises
and sings to the universe
who we are.

We are our grandmother's prayers.
We are our grandfather's dreamings.
We are the breath of our ancestors.
We are the spirit of God.

We are
Mothers of courage
Fathers of time
Daughters of dust
Sons of great vision.
We are
Sisters of mercy
Brothers of love
Lovers of life and
the builders of nations.
We are
Seekers of truth
Keepers of faith
Makers of peace and
the wisdom of ages.

We are our grandmother's prayers.
We are our grandfather's dreamings.

We are the breath of our ancestors.
We are the spirit of God.

For each child that's born
a morning star rises
and sings to the universe
who we are.

WE ARE ONE.

—Ysaye M. Barnwell © 1993

Profile Analysis

Ysaye Barnwell's story is an example of how easily talent or skill can be mistaken for a primary passion. At first glance, she seems to be someone whose Creator archetype is the major driver for all of her actions. She's a gifted singer, composer, and performer, who would seem to be living her passion through music. In fact, with an early childhood steeped in the music and culture born of the Harlem Renaissance period, one would expect that she'd choose to major in music in school and would have planned early on for the career she now enjoys.

When investigating her passions more deeply, we come to understand that the primary passion that motivates Ysaye is a passion for teaching. She gained early insight into this passion when assisting with her father's music lessons and later learning about the potential to teach the hearing impaired to speak. Typical of the Teacher archetype, she wants to impart knowledge and a love of learning to others. Interestingly, it is through teaching that she gives others a voice, to apply to their part of the chorus or to describe themselves to others. Her instrument is her voice, but her primary passion is to teach. Ysaye's Creator passion, as a result, becomes the mechanism for her Teacher passion to achieve its greatest impact.

Early in her career she pursued that passion in a traditional manner, by obtaining advanced degrees and positions in higher education. When life threw her a curve ball and she discovered that she wouldn't be offered a tenured job at Howard University, she surrendered her position but not her passions. Instead, Ysaye redirected the way in which her Teacher passion would be manifest, and she used her Creator passion and vocal gifts as a vehicle for its expression.

Through the work that she does with vocal communities, evidence of another of Ysaye's passions becomes apparent. She teaches through song and engages participants in the music by applying her Processor passion to analyze the song and deconstruct it into manageable pieces. In this way she is able to teach each member of the audience how to sing his or her respective part. Through her Processor passion, Ysaye takes the complexity of the music and makes it simpler and easily accessible for everyone.

Finally, this story illuminates one of the greatest desires of Teachers: to pass on the base of knowledge they possess. Ysaye willingly makes time in an intense and complex life to serve as a mentor to others. As a Teacher, her ultimate accomplishment is continuing the cycle of learning.

PART THREE

PUTTING PURPOSE AND
PASSION TO WORK

Awakening

The tonic of sleep
the power of mornings
the stillness they both hold
to reveal that opening in
the blackness that cloaks
our deepest desires
and grandest dreams
about our contribution to the world.
In the stillness,
in the quiet moments of the day
we peer through the portal
our eyes adjusting
to the brightness beyond . . .
the imagined possibilities
of our lives and our work
take form.

—*Alaina Love*

THIRTEEN

The Journey to Purpose and Passion

I FEEL THIS PANG INSIDE—
IS IT MY SOUL TRYING TO BREAK OUT,
OR THE WORLD'S SOUL TRYING TO BREAK IN?
—RABINDRANATH TAGORE

An Individual Quest

Over the last several years we've spent a great deal of time talking with people about purpose and passion. We've talked to all kinds of people, from college students to corporate executives, homemakers to entrepreneurs, folks with Ph.D.s and those with GEDs, the financially well off and the financially struggling. We've spoken to working men and women and to those who are unemployed. We've explored these concepts with Americans, Asians, Europeans, and Latin Americans. We've reached out to people with a variety of social, political, religious, and ethnic backgrounds. In short, we've talked with anyone willing to share their thoughts and anyone willing to listen.

The single unifying theme in all of these discussions is the desire that people have to live a life of substance, to identify and pursue their purpose and passions, and to find an outlet for them in their daily existence. Yes, people want to do work that matters; but they also want to do what matters to them at the deepest level. So an employee's desire for something more than just being satisfied with "doing well" in his or her career should really not be surprising.

The quest of individuals for purpose has been well documented throughout literature in any number of cultures, religions, and societies. It's a common theme in life and art that has spanned generations. Whether it was Elijah's quest to hear that "still small voice in the wind" that linked him to his higher calling or the wanderings of Homer's Odysseus as he struggled to return home to those elemental values that mattered most, to identify and live our purpose is a fundamental human need—a need that our focus in the workplace, filled with deadlines and obligations, objectives to meet, and profits to earn, leaves little time to address. When we realize that defining our purpose in concrete terms and deciding how to apply that purpose through work has the single greatest influence on shaping our future career and life decisions, the dichotomy becomes apparent. Purpose is the internal source of a well of creativity that can be tapped to address the most challenging business complexities or life adversities. Defining our purpose matters.

As we've spoken with individuals about purpose, we've sometimes encountered very skilled and successful people who were unable to answer the question, "How would you define your purpose in life?" You might think that an eight-word question with words no more than two syllables long couldn't possibly be too difficult for a talented executive to answer. After all, these are individuals who have managed billions of dollars in some of the most complex business environments on the planet. Yet, while many may have struggled with the answer, few were unaware of the importance of the question.

We've received all kinds of replies to this fundamental question. You might consider what yours would be if someone walked into the room right now and your life depended on knowing the answer. The responses we received have ranged from the general "My purpose in life is to be a good person" to the specific "I am a discoverer, and my purpose in life is to identify compounds that can eradicate disease and help humankind." From those who were less clear about their answer, we heard things like, "I don't know. I'm on my way to somewhere. I just hope I'll recognize it when I get there!" One might smile at that response and think it's rather simplistic, but there is a seed of truth buried within it. Identifying your purpose is indeed a journey, the length and complexity of which varies from person to person.

If you think that understanding individual purpose has no relevance to job satisfaction, think again. Employees' unhappiness with their work has given birth to the career-coaching phenomenon, currently a $1.5 billion industry worldwide.[1] The rising degree of employee unrest has created business for some 30,000 career coaches.[2] People are looking for insight and help with figuring out what they want to do at work. But more deeply rooted in developing an understanding about one's career plan is developing a more complete picture of one's major drivers in life. Our research and discussions with those who are on the journey have revealed an approach for accessing individual purpose and examining the passions that flow forth from it that is worth taking time to explore. While it's surely not the only technique for uncovering the answer to this deeply soul-based question, it is one that we have experienced personally and have seen work well for others. If you have discovered your Passion Archetypes Cluster by completing the Passion Profiler, this approach can provide further insight about applying your passions at work and in your personal life.

Preparing for the Journey

Before we can begin a discussion about an individual's journey to purpose, we must once again emphasize the fact that this is a journey, not a destination. What most individuals who are on this journey tell us is that signs of their purpose were revealed to them over time. Few leaped out of bed one morning with the thought in mind, "Ah, today will be the day I discover my purpose!" Surprisingly, however, many folks realized that signs of their purpose began to be revealed early on in life. On the journey to purpose, the past may not shape the future, but it can certainly inform it.

A good example of this is Dr. Steven Sims who is a senior research scientist for Whitmire Micro-Gen, one of the leading manufacturers and suppliers in the United States of general insect control products and equipment. Steve is an entomologist (a "bug guy") with a passion archetype of Discoverer. He studies insects for a living, and he works to find ways to effectively control infestation of food crops and animals. Steve loves exploring the unknown, and he knew that bugs would be his career from the time he was 19. As a child, he had been an avid collector of all kinds of insects, and by the time he was 7 years old, he realized that he enjoyed discovering new things in the natural world. (He later even earned a minor in botany.) A typical Discoverer, when working out a tough problem, Steve can be found in the lab at midnight; his purpose and passion keep him going when many of the rest of us are fast asleep.

Another important factor to keep in mind for the journey is that an outlet for your purpose may manifest in ways that you don't expect. A physician who attended one of our workshops for executives helped to highlight this point. Over the last few years, he had become increasingly disillusioned with his future career prospects. He had switched companies in search of a position about which he could feel excited for more than just a fleeting moment, but he was nervous about making too many more moves, fearful that it would negatively affect his career as well as his financial stability. With one child already in college and another not far behind, the executive felt forced to stay put in a job for which he had little passion. The company for which he was working had assigned him to a role outside of his field of specialty, and although he was doing a great job, something was still missing. He yearned for a role that held more meaning, although he couldn't at that time describe the ideal position.

Coupled with the dissatisfaction about his current role, the executive was working in a company that was in the middle of reorganization—for the third time in 18 months. He suspected that his department would be caught in the restructuring and that his job, along with those reporting to him, would ultimately be affected. While his bosses reassured him that he was a "valued asset" to the company, they continued to suggest new positions for him in which he had little interest. But this talented executive, with bills to pay and children to educate, continued to say no, all the while holding his breath because he couldn't identify a position about which he could say yes. However, when we asked him to describe the positions that he had most enjoyed in the past, they all included one common characteristic—having an opportunity to teach and mentor others.

After a good deal of reflection during and after the workshop, it began to dawn on this executive that his purpose in life was to teach. In fact, he realized it was his passion, and he could point to numerous times in the past when he had joyfully found a way to teach, regardless of his job title or level in an organization. The physician was even able to describe how his purpose carried over to his personal life. One day, his teenaged son asked him about how car engines worked. Instead of providing the boy with a simplistic answer or encouraging him to read about it in a book, the physician drove to a local junkyard and purchased an old engine. Head to head, he and his son spent hours bent over the old engine while the father happily explained the intricacies of gas-fired combustion. He loved having an opportunity to teach!

Unfortunately, the physician's current role at work offered little opportunity for that passion. Because of the current reorganization, it increasingly began to seem that finding what he wanted would require leaving the organization. But about six weeks after the workshop, he called to discuss a surprising new offer he'd received from the company. Senior management wanted him to take a lead role in medical education for a major division, a position with an outlet for both his purpose and his skills. All of his searching and determination to find a meaningful role had finally paid off; and amidst the chaos of multiple reorganizations, the reward came when he least expected it.

To management's credit, they had some sense of the executive's value to the organization, but they had no idea of how to capitalize on his potential. They spent more than a year offering the physician roles that were anything but a good fit for his purpose and passion. In the process, they paid a hefty price for this mistake. They had a highly compensated employee on the payroll who was not fully engaged. He drove to work in the morning tuned into music to drown out the day ahead, and every evening he drove home the same way. This changed once he was placed in the right position; the executive then spent hours of personal time thinking about his work and relishing the challenges of each new assignment. Considering the opportunity cost, this was clearly a situation in which the employee's contribution should have been maximized much earlier in the game. Luckily for the employee and the organization, an outlet for his passion appeared just in time.

Defining an Approach for Accessing Purpose and Passion

What we've learned from personal experience and from the talented individuals we've interviewed is that the journey to purpose for many of us can be summarized in a four-step approach that we call **PREP** (*Prep*aring for the Journey):

Present and Open
Reflect and Partner
Examine
Persist

Rather than being an attempt to distill a complex analysis of life and work into an overly simplistic formula, **PREP** can be thought of more accurately as a framework for action that can help us navigate through critical questions and the answers to them that give meaning to our lives. **PREP** requires that we be Present and Open on the journey and recognize that it is the daily experience of engaging in meaningful activities that helps us to define our purpose and create the outlets for the passions that spring forth from it. The focus for the journey is on being in the now. By doing so, we do not limit our thinking about how purpose and passion will manifest or obsess about the future; instead, we recognize that opportunities to express it may arise in surprising ways, like the passionate physician/teacher whose company unexpectedly offered him a position in education.

Reflect and Partner, the second and most essential step of the approach, refers to utilizing four important ingredients for the journey: Stillness, Contemplation, Courage, and Community. These ingredients are so critical to achieving and living our purpose and passions that we will spend the balance of this chapter exploring them.

Examine, the third step in the approach, requires that we take a good, hard look at our past for what it reveals about our purpose and passions. This step asks us to consider some fundamental questions about past experiences in our work and personal lives that might provide clues about how to build a life driven by passion and purpose in the present. It also asks us to consider what we are willing to do in the present to shape that life. Will we shift from complaining about the circumstances of the present to actively constructing a meaningful future?

Finally, when we Persist in the pursuit of purpose, we recognize that journeys are rarely a straight line from point *A* to point *B*. Invariably, most paths are filled with turns, detours, and unexpected forks in the road. These can sometimes lead to discouragement, disillusionment, or fatigue, any of which can get the best of us if we let it. Maintaining our footing on the path to purpose requires our willingness to weather the tough times while pursuing our ideals. Persistence is what helps us stay the course.

By now you've discovered your Passion Archetype Cluster. This is your opportunity to use what you've learned about your archetypes to uncover the purpose at the heart of those passions as you progress through the **PREP** process.

The Key Ingredients for Step II

The key ingredients that comprise Step II, Reflect and Partner, deserve special attention because they are the limiting reagent in the complex set of reactions that lead to understanding individual purpose, without which the journey ceases. There are four important ingredients in the recipe: Stillness, Contemplation, Courage, and Community. These are leavening to the baker, those elements that help purpose rise up within us.

To describe the interplay between these ingredients in the deciphering of your purpose, it might be helpful to consider them as analogous to the four dimensions of our universe described by early physicists. These dimensions (one time and three spatial dimensions) are independent components that must interact together in a specific way for structure as we know it to exist or for an event to take place. The same is true of the ingredients for purpose; they too are interde-

AN APPROACH FOR ACCESSING PURPOSE AND PASSION

STEP	ACTION(S)	DISCOVERIES
I	Present and Open	IT IS IMPORTANT TO RECOGNIZE THE PROCESS AS A JOURNEY RATHER THAN A DESTINATION. Living your purpose and passions is not about arriving at a specific point; rather, it is about enjoying the daily experience of engaging in meaningful activities that provide you with a sense of fulfillment and an opportunity to create a positive legacy. For many people, the journey may be a process that unfolds throughout their entire lives, and the various stages of the journey are shaped by the wealth of work and life experience they obtain. An outlet for your purpose and passions may manifest in a way that you don't expect. It is important to stay open to opportunities; even those that don't seem like obvious routes may lead you to your destination.
II	Reflect and Partner	THE FOUR IMPORTANT INGREDIENTS FOR THE JOURNEY ARE STILLNESS, CONTEMPLATION, COURAGE, AND COMMUNITY. Because this is the most critical step in the approach, it is essential to understand these ingredients and apply them in your daily activities. And, if you are a leader, creating space for them in the work environment is instrumental in developing a purpose-focused culture in the organization. We discuss more about these important ingredients later in this chapter and in Chapter 14.
III	Examine	EXAMINING THE PAST FOR SIGNS AND SIGNALS OF PURPOSE AND PASSION MAY PROVIDE NEW ENLIGHTENMENT. Examining ourselves helps to reveal what we are willing to do to create a fulfilling life. Look for the sources of joy and excitement that past work assignments or life experiences may reveal. Start with your past work roles, but don't limit your thinking. Roles that you've played in

AN APPROACH FOR ACCESSING PURPOSE AND PASSION

STEP	ACTION(S)	DISCOVERIES
		your private life might also hold some important clues. Look deeply within yourself to identify just how much you are willing to do to construct a life filled with purpose and passion. Some important questions to consider are these: • When did you feel most alive in your work? What were the features of the roles you most enjoyed? • What was the environment that provided you with a sense of openness, expansion, and possibility? • What were the characteristics of the community of people you interacted with that contributed to your sense of fulfillment? • Are there volunteer activities you've engaged in that have been particularly satisfying? What were they, and why were they meaningful to you? • How committed are you presently to shaping a life of purpose with an outlet for your passions? Are you willing to do the work to make this a reality?
IV	Persist	SOME JOURNEYS TAKE LONGER THAN OTHERS. All of them are filled with twists and turns and occasional dead ends. Looking at these challenges as learning experiences enriches the journey and informs your thinking. Persistence is a strong ally in the lifelong process of living authentically.

pendent concepts that contribute to the shape and structure of our work and private lives.

For example, a lack of Stillness can hamper our ability to contemplate, or at a minimum it can severely impair the quality of our thinking. Stillness and Contemplation are separate components; yet they are interdependent in their support of the journey's outcome.

Courage too is a requirement for the journey. Understanding the difference between Courage and foolhardiness is developed through Contemplation—an act of kindness we extend to ourselves when we take time to connect with our deepest thoughts and insights.

Likewise, the journey is supported by Community; but the type of Community we find ourselves most at home in is as much a function of our individual progress toward purpose as it is a function of the joint development of those around us. We do not travel this path in isolation. Our expression of purpose (and its outward demonstration as passion) impacts others, as we too are touched, shaped, and informed by their journey.

The map for the journey to purpose and passion is far more complex than the route that can be programmed on your car's navigation system. There is no defined starting point at which we each must begin. How you need to approach the journey may differ from how another highly successful colleague goes about it. What's important is to find your own starting place and enter the journey from there.

Creating the Right Mix for Purpose and Passion: The Art of Reflecting and Partnering

Ingredients 1 and 2:
Valuing Stillness and Contemplation

We will examine Ingredients 1 and 2 together because they are so intimately connected. Stillness is the elixir for Contemplation, the quieting of the mind and body, the cessation of action that creates a space for new ideas and concepts to reside. Without Stillness, no act of Contemplation can be initiated; there is simply no opening through which the objects of our potential Contemplation might enter our consciousness. Contemplation depends on the portal for ideas that Stillness provides, without which the entrée of new concepts is impossible.

Unfortunately, Stillness is counterintuitive in the traditional corporate model, a model whose dominant feature is constant motion. The results-focused culture of many organizations creates an almost pathological need to be doing *something,* even when we are unsure that the movement we're making will bring about the desired outcome. When we are not still, we believe that we are perceived as doing our part to realize the collective goal, which in turn only feeds the existing pathology. With this first important ingredient absent on the list of traditional strategic options, organizations and their employees erroneously regard Stillness as time wasted, and "time is money," isn't it? Since no one wants to be typed as a "slacker," workers make an effort to look busy even if they yearn for, and need, quiet time.

A country manager in the Philippines, working for a major multinational company, shared a story about his driver that highlights the extent to which this pathology has become part of the collective psyche: "He was an excellent driver, safe and reliable, but he had one flaw. He seemed to feel that he was not doing his job unless the wheels of the car were turning. Each night on the way home, we would cross the permanently jammed main road out of the business district to hurtle through a maze of broadly parallel residential streets. We would then rejoin the main road closer to the set of lights that permitted us to cross an even busier road to get into my village. After a while, I started to make note of the license plate of the car in front as it turned onto the main road, while my driver dove into the maze in an attempt to avoid the traffic. About 90 percent of the time we emerged from our frenzied dash to rejoin the main road directly behind the same vehicle now waiting at the lights!" Clearly, taking time for Stillness and Contemplation may save wear and tear on your car; in the work environment it may also save wear and tear on your mind.

A New Business Practice?

While the practice of Stillness and Contemplation may seem to have no rightful place or value in the competitive business environment, more and more executives are engaging in this practice. One such executive, Vijay Eswaran, the CEO of the Hong Kong–based QI Group, begins each morning with an hour in silent contemplation. Vijay is a Hindu Indian born in Malaysia who runs a near-billion-dollar telecommunications, entertainment, and e-commerce conglomerate. The

QI enterprise includes a variety of intensely competitive businesses in 30 countries, including a private mint in Germany, TV stations in Europe and Dubai, and investments in publicly traded companies in Sri Lanka and India, as well as telecommunications companies and resorts. It is not a business for the faint hearted.

Vijay learned about Stillness and Contemplation from his grandfather, whose entire household would go silent for an hour each day. *Mouna*, or Stillness, is a tradition in India, generally practiced during *brahmamuhurta*, the two hours before sunrise. This is the time that represents the birth of the new day. Vijay describes *mouna* as "a highly individual vigorous mental workout," and he believes it is a practical approach to life in a fast, demanding, chaotic world. From a business perspective, Vijay uses this time to prepare for the day and review the problems that need to be solved. In his form of the practice, he pins down where he wants to go in work and life by writing down 8 to 12 objectives for the day. "On a good day, I achieve maybe 6 of them," he said. "*Mouna* reminds you of a greater purpose beyond just the day ahead of you. Something you do today should have significance a year or more from now. This practice keeps me on track. It's like a compass bearing." On a higher level, *mouna* also provides him with an opportunity to commune spiritually and connect with the most important questions in his heart.

Vijay believes that taking time for *mouna* allows him to gain a multidimensional perspective about the challenges of the business and improves his mental fitness. A great number of his employees have also begun to use this practice prior to coming to the office each day. The results can be seen in the company's retention rates, which are higher than the norm, especially among senior leaders. Vijay also believes that company loyalty has increased among other workers; they demonstrate a passion for the business and the 3.5 million customers that the QI Group serves. "Involving purpose as part of business objectives is critical," he emphatically stated.

On a practical level, Vijay taps back into *mouna* periodically during the day to reconnect to his goals. Prior to intense meetings where discussions may be challenging, he slips away to the office washroom to grab a few moments of silence. "It just takes a couple of minutes to review my plan for the meeting and set my intent. I think about what I want to achieve, where I want to go, and what my purpose is at this moment," said Vijay. He jokes that he suspects his staff thinks he has digestive problems because slipping away to the men's room just before meetings has become such a ritual for him.

When others characterize his business approach as New Age nonsense, Vijay responds, "It works. Most of my people are on a course that resonates with what we do and who they are. At the end of the day, if they're not giving as much in mental creativity as they are in physical work, then the profits aren't going to pan out. But the organization itself has to realize that it needs a greater purpose, the kind that extends beyond just money. When employees have grown as people and can handle greater responsibilities, I see *that* as profit."

Leaders would be wise to recognize that practiced Stillness in the business environment is not time wasted; it is thought in creation. Establishing time for Stillness in the day provides space for the intuitive to take up residence in our linear, logical world. And the intuitive, as well as logic, can lead to great insights. Just consider Einstein, arguably one of the most brilliant minds of the last century. He frequently spent time in Stillness and Contemplation in order to solve the complex puzzles of our universe. On more than one occasion he described his deepest insights as having originated from intuition.[3]

Each of us has natural access to the intuitive, an ability hardwired into our complex genome. Some of us access it through meditation or, like Vijay, through *mouna*, when we practice quieting our minds and bodies while opening ourselves to new insights. Most of us spend hours each night exploring through sleep the inner recesses of the intuitive as we process the prior day, replay events in search of new outcomes, and explore new solutions to old troubles in our dreams. Through sleep, meditation, and Stillness, we may venture into the intuitive and connect to our purpose.

Taking Time for Meaning Making

For some students of purpose, early mornings may be best for Stillness and Contemplation. As we emerge from the ephemeral nighttime world, we remain attached to a delicate thread, the umbilical cord to the deep knowing with which we enter the day. The cord is a fragile one, easily shattered by too much sound or movement. Like those practicing *mouna* in India, entering our day slowly and with reverence may be to our advantage, while the fragile cord is still intact and the lessons of the night fresh within us.

As we've learned from this ancient practice, the silent, contemplative moments of the day are to be revered and protected—from the intrusion of others, from the senseless chatter of meaningless meetings, and from the shrill, incessant demands of the telephone and other electronic devices that govern our work existence. These moments can be found on either end of the day—dawn or dusk, or wedged someplace between. What's important is to construct them as part of your daily plan. Turn off the phone, put the BlackBerry in the desk drawer, and disconnect from the rest of the world. Whether you start with five minutes a day or an hour doesn't matter. Just begin at your beginning.

So many of us become immersed in the daily rigors of the workday world, and we would say that there is little time for the luxury of Stillness and Contemplation. We think that we must be constantly available by phone or e-mail or in person, and we fail to recognize the importance of scheduling a meeting with ourselves. We give most of our time to other things and other people in an effort to achieve. So over the years, we tend to measure our lives by our achievements because they are the only tangible currencies we have. Immortal in our youth, more settled in our thirties, perhaps bored with the routine of the repetitive business cycle by our forties, by not making time for Stillness and Contemplation, many of us risk spending nearly 20 years of our work life not fully immersed in the now and confused about what holds meaning for us. We tell ourselves that one day we'll carve out time to contemplate the journey. We wait for tomorrows, next months, or next quarters, and we measure our progress toward some "important" goal that results only in yet another goal that must be achieved. Too often we do not make use of the time that we have to explore the wholeness of ourselves and our work. We are then left wondering how a career that started with such promise becomes a source of so much discontent.

This is a state of being not limited by age, race, or gender. Individuals would do well to recognize that squandered Stillness is not a midcareer disease but an equal opportunity infection. People of all backgrounds, including younger workers, should heed the early signs of discontent with their work and pause to seek a better connection with their inner core. Stillness and Contemplation, used well, make up the route to that connection.

The Art of Contemplation

Those new to the concepts of Stillness and Contemplation may wonder what it is they're supposed to be doing during this time. It's not easy for individuals accustomed to a daily ride on the hard-driving, fast-moving conveyor belt of the workday world to step off for a moment of Contemplation. Many are fearful that the belt will move on without them and they'll lose their place in line. But much can be gained by taking this time. It can improve our ability to function at work by helping us to develop a greater understanding of ourselves and our influence on the world around us.

For some, this time is best used by sitting and quietly reflecting. Others we have spoken with tell us that writing down the questions they most need answers to and the thoughts they receive in reply helps them to gain greater insight about the path forward. Some individuals use this time to process their challenges at work or home and search for meaning within them. Still others utilize this time by hiking in the woods, jogging alone, or reading inspiring passages from a book. One young ex-Marine we know, who is now a manager for the Mars corporation (think M&Ms and Snickers candies), insists that his most contemplative time occurs when he is working out alone in the local gym. Keeping his body occupied with weight lifting, he says, allows his mind to quiet, so that at the same time he is strengthening his body, he is also processing his problems and searching for meaning in his life.

What we learn from this wide variety of approaches is that it is not important to use a defined prescription for accessing Stillness and engaging in Contemplation. What *is* important is to consistently use an approach that works for you, one that ideally allows you to limit the range of what you think about so that you can focus on what really matters. This process is about stilling the chatter in your mind long enough to allow new insight to enter.

So what informs our thinking most during these times of Contemplation? What will help us gain the greatest insight into the path forward? Based on our research, using Contemplation to facilitate an understanding of our purpose is an in → out and out → in process. In the first form of reflection, we learn by intensely examining ourselves. Through this process of inward focus, we develop our own philosophy of life and a set of convictions by which we live it; we develop the personal values that guide our behaviors; we begin to forge a connection between our personal interests and career interests; and we gain a greater understanding of our role in the relationships that we share with others. In brief, this learning-from-within process is a mode of deep reflective thinking that helps us make meaning of our world by supporting our understanding of who we are, what we believe, and what we value and aspire to in life.

Likewise, the out → in reflective process is indicative of the learning that we gain by external experiences, which we process internally to provide us with greater insight. Individuals who make use of this outward-focused mechanism allow events in the work environment to prompt them to think in reflective ways. For these individuals, work experiences are a way to garner a comprehensive understanding of their strengths and vulnerabilities so that they can seek ways to apply that knowledge to set goals for their further development and career growth. Through work, they are also able to refine their values by utilizing challenging experiences to help test and internalize those values in a significant way. Individuals who use outward-focused Contemplation may also find that they connect to society through their work or that their work helps to clarify the importance of establishing this connection. At the highest levels of reflective thinking, the focus for individuals shifts from one centered on themselves to one centered on the impact they can have on humanity as a whole. Both contemplative processes facilitate this more inclusive perspective.

In his book *Choosing to Choose*, futurist and social psychologist Avrom E. King highlighted some important responsibilities that we might examine during these moments of intense reflection, especially in the context of our relationships with others. As can be seen in the following table, each of these responsibilities evokes questions that can serve as an initial focal point for reflective Contemplation.

The responsibilities that King defined have relevance to all mature relationships. In the business environment, these responsibilities extend to our roles at work as well; examining them can enhance what we learn about ourselves and what we learn about our purpose. When we apply these same responsibilities (and the questions they evoke) to our work relationships, we learn that operating from a place of purpose is to our advantage and to the advantage of the organization.

RESPONSIBILITIES TO BE REFLECTED UPON

RESPONSIBILITIES	QUESTIONS FOR REFLECTION
To be pure in our motives	Am I acting from a place of highest good when I interact with others?
To demonstrate integrity in our actions	Am I working at all times and with all people from a place of honesty and candor?
To tell those with whom we're in a relationship how we really feel	Am I openly sharing my true thoughts and feelings, or am I expecting others to guess about them? When they don't guess correctly, am I holding it against them?
To tell others what we want	In my communication with others, am I clear about my desires? Do I compromise my needs in the moment and then feel resentful about it later?

Adapted from Avrom E. King, *Choosing to Choose*, Dharma Publishing, Phoenix, 1998.

For example, when operating "on purpose" at work, our motives are pure, so we act for the good of others and the company but we do not sacrifice our own highest good in the process. In staying true to ourselves, we gain the added benefit of forging a stronger link to our purpose. Likewise, when purpose is the guide for our behaviors at work, we're honest and candid with our colleagues, customers, and community. We're also straightforward with our leaders, and we provide them with our unfiltered input. Accepting our responsibilities means that we bring forth the good news and the bad in a timely way, so that action can be taken when needed. We also welcome input from others who operate in the same way. Finally, contemplating our responsibilities and the questions that accompany them gives us insight into what we want and expect from work relationships and helps us to share our desires with others. In doing so, we willingly hold ourselves accountable to work from a place of purpose and ask others, and the organization, to do the same.

Ingredient 3: Working with Courage

A number of the executives we interviewed indicated that understanding and embodying their purpose required forfeiting the model of who they are that others had defined for them. Awakening to purpose necessitated an intense letting go, releasing the need for complete order and predictability, and relinquishing the need to know all of the answers. They learned that the journey is instead a process of immersing oneself in the questions. And it's a journey that requires Courage. They had to be willing to bravely venture into the chaos of their own inner uncertainties and ask: Am I in the right job? Is my work fulfilling my soul as much as it is my wallet? What will my family think about me if I choose to leave the organization, or stay? And what will I think about myself? By navigating through the primordial soup of who they are and where they fit in, these courageous executives gathered the knowledge that helped to reveal their purpose, and they learned how to apply it in the context of their daily work.

Sometimes there were dark moments when even the most talented among them were challenged during the journey. And it often happened when they had achieved all that they had imagined in their careers. They were occupying the very position they had coveted, only to find the accomplishment made them miserable. For several executives, this was the single greatest moment of personal transformation— the moment they began to realize that their true self had somehow become lost inside the corporation. But this moment provided the greatest opportunity for change and growth, both for the individuals and their organizations. It was also the moment of greatest risk, when their Courage and intent were tested as they fought to move forward in their lives with authenticity and integrity.

While working with these executives, we encountered a talented and successful leader at just such a point in his career, when marshaling Courage became critical. "Lee" had built businesses for an international manufacturing company throughout Eastern Europe, and he had created high-powered teams to lead them. In just seven years, he had developed nine profitable subsidiaries in a market in which the company previously had limited presence. He had negotiated lucrative deals for the organization in some of the most challenging business environments and created a strong brand presence in the region. In short, this was an executive that made things happen.

At some point in his career, the company decided to bring Lee back to a headquarters job, without first considering his core needs for fulfillment and satisfaction. In the new role, he began to find himself less and less comfortable with the corporate costume he was now required to wear. The fit became tighter each day as Lee's inner certainty about his purpose blossomed. Over time, the organization began to appreciate him less and less, and Lee began to feel unwelcome and undervalued.

Some months after assuming this new position, Lee walked into our office holding a printout from a test he had taken over the Internet. Unbelievably, it was an IQ test on which he had scored 149—bordering on genius territory. "Why," we asked, "did you take such a test?" Given his track record of accomplishment, we could not imagine the need to do so. Our experience with Lee had been filled with exciting conversations, thoughtful discussions on the approach to the market and the development of his team, along with entertaining stories of his adventures in less developed areas of the region, where squawking chickens and howling dogs were cabin companions on flights to remote areas.

On this visit to our office, we saw Lee's mask of feigned confidence fall away. Gone were the humor and the light in his eyes. This talented man took a deep breath and swallowed audibly before he answered. Tears were welling up in his eyes, the raw vulnerability of someone not accustomed to uncertainty and fear. He quietly replied, "I wasn't sure of myself anymore. I'm beginning to think that my past success was just dumb luck and that maybe they're right not to want me here anymore."

Lee eventually left his company, and the organization struggled with leadership in his region for many years. He took some time to plan his next career move and, as he told us, "took time to heal." Since then, Lee has gone on to even greater success with another organization, but he is careful now to choose work that resonates with his purpose, where he can bring the whole of who he is to his work. This leader's story highlights the fact that facing fear on the path to purpose is an important part of the journey, but it is also perhaps the most difficult—and Courage may be our only ally. It is the activator that brings purpose into the bold light of day. We learn that living our purpose courageously is living with integrity.

Working with purpose and passion then, becomes a visible example of self-respect, an honoring of our gifts. Toiling away day after day or year after year at a role that we find mind-numbing, about which we feel little passion, is disrespectful to the soul as well as the organization. It's an act that limits us. We waste those precious, fleeting, unrecoverable hours of the day, steeped in responsibilities devoid of joy, disconnected from our passion and the whole of ourselves. Finding an outlet for purpose and passion in our work is the only certain conduit for emerging from this predicament.

In the best of organizational cultures, there is appreciation for all of the ingredients necessary for employee purpose to blossom. But perhaps the greatest contribution that organizations can make to an individual's quest for purpose is in offering space and acceptance for Courage, which can be sourced only from the individual. In fact, the need for the kind of creative inspiration that leads to innovation in the marketplace will require that companies embrace and support Courage and the people who are willing to demonstrate it.

Detours on the Journey

How is it that some of us venture so far from the passion in our work? What are the seductions that we pursue in favor of nurturing the ideals that were born of our purpose and brought us to the job in the first place? In brief, we lose perspective. We experience success, and in doing so, we redefine success as the trappings of the corporate stage. Our lives become marked by our achievements and the outward recognition we receive for them: the travels to exotic places on the corporate jet; the new cars and luxury possessions; the corner office with a important title; the salary and stock options that put us in the highest tax bracket; the press releases about ourselves that we begin to believe; and the awe and admiration we receive from others. Like mainlined heroin, it courses through our veins imparting euphoria never before experienced, until the day the syringe can't be filled full enough to overcome the descent when the drug tapers off.

It is at this moment that we have a choice to shift our position from corporate soldier to corporate renegade. If we choose a position on the sidelines, we've chosen no position at all. But if we choose the path of the renegade, a wide-open field is available to us. This is a path we best travel with purpose firmly in hand, prepared and well-armed for the courageous journey ahead to find a home within, rather than outside, the organization. And as renegades, we must suspend attachments to the seductions of the corporate suite, instead staying close to the roots of our existence, as we are reminded by poet David Whyte:

> To live with courage in any work or any organization, we
> must know intimately the part of us that does not give a damn
> about the organization or the work. That knows how to live
> outside the law as well as within it. We do this not to create
> a veneer of protection through cynicism, but so that we can
> meet the powerful structures that inform our existence on
> equal terms. In a conversation of equals, there is all to play for.

*Something can occur that neither side could anticipate; pre-
dictability, routinization, boredom, and powerlessness are all
in abeyance. With a healthy outlaw approach, we are outside
the laws of predictable cause and effect and inside the intensity
of creative originality.*[4]

Ingredient 4: The Power of Community

From the earliest of civilizations, Community with others was a central component necessary for survival. Whether it's the antelope on the
African plain or a herd of mares in Wyoming protecting their foals,
animals have long been aware of the importance of Community. Human beings, likewise, find safety in numbers and a sense of belonging
that feeds the soul. Through the power of Community, groups work
to accomplish collective goals, be it the growth of revenue in the corporate world or the building of the hive for the honeybee, Community
with others makes it all possible.

As we travel the path toward full expression of purpose, we find
comfort and support in the company of others. But through this journey we become more than independent contributors to the larger
landscape. The very act of making the journey itself shifts the environment experienced by the whole work Community so that along
with others it is possible to cocreate a new reality. A linear corporate
culture can be shifted to a door-thrust-open-on-a-windy-day culture
of fresh creativity. Together with the larger work Community, operating from purpose helps individuals to define a new edge, beyond
where past boundaries ended. From this vantage point emerges a new
understanding of what the business can be.

Organizations would do well to acknowledge the value of Community on this sometimes challenging journey to purpose because
it is through others that employees hone and craft their message. In
sharing their stories and metaphors, they help their colleagues to understand their purpose and passions and make space for them in daily
work relationships. The Community of coworkers honors one another
simply through the act of listening. They support purpose by respect-
ing one another's gifts and by witnessing the outcome of doing so—

work done with authenticity, work done with the wholeness of the organization and customer in mind, . . . work done with joy.

Moving toward purpose and passion, therefore, becomes an act of choosing joy in our work and in all other aspects of our existence. When we allow the passion within us to be reawakened and applied to our work, we enthusiastically seek unique answers to the organization's challenges and push the edges of creative boundary in partnership with those with whom we share the journey. This larger Community of work partners sustains us in our effort to move purpose and passion from being limited internal constructs to having a rightful place in the open dialogue of the organization. Our work partners cheer us on, inspired by our passion and heartened by the refreshing changes to the culture that it produces. In walking our bold path forward, we blaze a trail for others to follow.

 FOURTEEN

Getting Results through Purpose and Passion

MOST PEOPLE BRING THREE KINDS OF NEEDS TO THEIR
ORGANIZATIONAL EXISTENCE: A NEED TO BE REWARDED [TANGIBLY]
FOR WHAT THEY ACHIEVE, A NEED TO BE ACCEPTED AS A UNIQUE
PERSON, AND A NEED TO BE APPRECIATED NOT ONLY FOR THE
FUNCTION PERFORMED BUT ALSO AS A HUMAN BEING.
—RICHARD TANNER PASCALE

We hope that the previous chapters of this book have created a compelling case for the importance of awakening employees' internal purpose and fostering its external expression as passions that can be applied to the work of the organization. For those who may still be a bit skeptical, we'd like to offer several perspectives that will cement the value of connecting with employee purpose and passion and its impact on organizational results. We'll begin by examining the issue from the cultural perspective, and we'll move on to a practical review of how leveraging individual and team passions drives results, supports strategies, grows knowledge, and gets the right people in the right seats on the bus. Finally, we'll introduce an easily installed process that can be adapted to organizational systems to support efforts to maximize employee passions at work.

The Impact of Culture on Leveraging Purpose and Passion

In our early research with high-potential talent, where we explored the importance that individuals placed on finding an outlet for their purpose and passions at work, we asked study participants about what changes they would recommend for their own organizations to support achieving this outcome. One of the most frequently recommended changes suggested was to restructure the culture of the organization to one that encourages employees to pursue their purpose at work so that fulfillment is achieved throughout their careers.

That got us thinking and wondering about what framework could be defined for accomplishing the cultural shift that study participants suggested. What simple construct could we identify to describe the way in which a culture must operate in order to create an environment where employees bring the best of themselves to work each day and apply it to achieving outstanding results? And could this culture make a difference not only in employee engagement and fulfillment but also in the kind of productivity and decision making that leads to great business results? Interestingly, the answer came to us from the field of behavioral economics.

Dr. Dan Ariely, a behavioral economist and Duke University professor, has spent his career working to discover what makes us tick from a behavioral point of view when it relates to the economic decisions we make, such as what we'll purchase and what rewards we're willing to work for. We spoke to Dan about some of the elegant research he has conducted on market norm and social norm–based human behavior, which he outlines in his book *Predictably Irrational*.

Among the large body of work he has amassed on the subject, one particular analysis stood out for us. Dan outlined a series of experiments that he and University of St. Thomas professor James Heyman conducted to determine the relative impact of social and market norms on the amount of labor participants would be willing to put into a job. In their experiment, participants sat at a computer screen and were asked to drag a circle on one side of the screen into a square on the other. Participants were paid based on the number of times they completed this task. Ariely and Heyman applied two levels of compensation with the first two groups of participants they tested, offering one group 50 cents for each successfully completed task and the other group 10 cents for doing the same task. As might be expected, the group that was paid 50 cents per task dragged roughly 50 percent more circles into the squares than did the group paid the lower wage. In this instance, market norm thinking prevailed—the more participants were paid, the harder they worked. No surprises there.

But an interesting twist to the experiment was implemented when the participants in a third group were asked to perform the task as a social request. They were not offered money or any other form of compensation; instead, they were asked to perform the act as a favor. Surprisingly, the third group of participants worked significantly harder than either of the others that were paid for their services! Apparently, being asked to volunteer their services resulted in these participants putting in so much extra effort that they outperformed their paid counterparts.

Imagine the power of social norms in the work environment! These experiments show that it is possible to motivate individuals to work—and work harder than others who are being paid a wage—by tapping into social norm thinking.

Now you might wonder whether this experiment turned out the way it did simply because Ariely and Heyman were working with a relatively low effort task that participants might be willing to engage in without pay. What would happen if a group of professionals were asked to charge a lower fee for providing their services if the request was to support a needy cause? Would they do it? If so, how much less would they charge?

Interestingly, an example exists in which these questions were answered. Ariely described a situation in which the AARP requested that some attorneys offer their services to needy retirees at a reduced rate. However, the lawyers refused to do so. Undaunted, a savvy manager went back to the attorneys and asked if they would instead offer their services for free. To this request, the preponderance of lawyers said yes. Not an expected result! When the attorneys had an opportunity to earn *something* for their services (albeit less than their going rate), they refused to reduce their fees, but when they were asked to perform the same work for free, many in the group said yes.

It all boils down to the lens through which the request was viewed.

Behavioral economics indicate that when we're asked to reduce our service fees, our thought processes function against the set of expectations that we carry about our perceived market value. We're just not willing to work for less than we believe we're worth because we operate from a "market norm perspective." But something interesting happens when we're suddenly asked to donate our services. It's similar to what occurs when a friend has a flat tire and asks for our help to change it. Most of us wouldn't dream of demanding pay for doing what we perceive to be a "Good Samaritan" favor for someone else. In this situation, our thinking adopts a "social norm perspective" in which we associate our services with doing a good deed for someone in need. Our expected "compensation" for our services shifts from a monetary form to become instead the sense of fulfillment we gain from the thought of helping someone else, and the warm glow generated by their appreciation.

The shift between market norm thinking and social norm thinking that human beings exhibit presents an interesting perspective about the competitive power of purpose and passion in the workplace. Imagine if organizations could somehow trigger more social norm thinking in their employees, so that workers would be willing to "donate" more of their time to achieving business goals. Now, we're not suggesting here that employees could be coerced into working for free, but we are proposing that there is interplay between market norm and social norm thinking that impacts organizational culture. And it's a competitive force that savvy organizations can tap into. Let's explore the dynamics of that relationship further.

The interplay between market norms and social norms depicted in Figure 14.1 suggests that there is in fact an opportunity that organizations can leverage. Here we see the stream of individual development driven by market norms compared to individual development

FIGURE 14.1 IMPACT OF PASSION ON
ORGANIZATIONAL CULTURE

Individual Development Driven by Market Norms

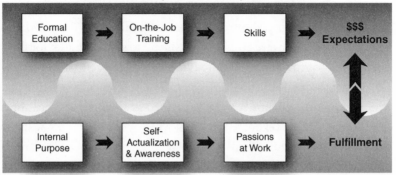

Individual Development Driven by Social Norms

driven by a social norm framework. In a culture that functions from a market norm perspective (one that most of us have grown up in), people are encouraged to obtain a formal education that will prepare them for the work environment. Once they obtain a job, workers are expected to continue their learning through on-the-job training and experience, which ultimately leads to the development of new skills or the enhancement of skills obtained through formal education. Market norm thinking in this group of workers would define an expectation to be financially compensated for gaining and applying skills. The more experience and skill obtained, the greater the expectation for reward—more money, a larger office, a more important title, reserved parking, stock options, and bonus eligibility are all forms of entitlement driven by a market norm–focused culture. The contractual arrangement (written or understood) between employees and their company is that the workers deliver results for which the company compensates them in cash or cash equivalents. The greater the results produced, the more those workers' skills are developed and the greater the expectation among those workers for increasing levels of reward.

But is this the only way in which organizations can achieve results through their people? Is it possible that social norm forces could be brought to bear on employee performance? How might social norm thinking impact the way in which organizations achieve sustainable changes to the culture to support future success?

In the social norm context depicted in Figure 14.1, individuals arrive in the world hardwired with an internal purpose. Over time, through exploration and introspection, the individuals (the workers) become more self-aware and are more likely to seek an outlet for their purpose. Since much of the individuals' learning occurs through experiences at work, the job setting becomes a potential avenue through which individual purpose can be expressed as work-related passions. The "compensation" expected by employees operating within a social norm framework shifts from a singular focus on financial reward to an interplay between monetary reward and the sense of personal fulfillment achieved through work.

In a holistic organizational culture, where a balance exists between market norm and social norm thinking, the benefits are many. The organization achieves a level of performance from its employees that far exceeds the financial investment the organization is making in the workers, and the workers achieve a level of fulfillment through their work beyond what typical financial rewards can provide. The connectedness that employees feel to their work and the organization leads to better business decisions. In a holistic culture, leadership decision making is likely to take on a focus that is longer term than the quarter-to-quarter perspective that is so common in many organizations today. And when leaders and employees are focused on the legacy they'll leave behind, they will be less likely to sell out the future for a temporary gain for the current moment. Instead of solely pursuing success, they are striving for significance. This is a culture powered for results.

There are a variety of factors that an organization must have in place to support adequate interplay between market and social norm thinking. The first and most important is the organization's acknowledgment of the value of the totality that employees bring to the business. They arrive at work each day with a set of skills, for sure, but employees also bring with them a deeply internalized purpose that can be observed in the passions they'll exhibit—if given the opportunity to do so.

The workers continually make personal investments in both streams of their own development. In the market norm stream, for example, they invest time and money to be educated to gain knowledge that can be applied at work. In the social norm stream, on the other hand, individuals invest emotion and spirit to discover their core drivers and determine the interface between those drivers and their work roles. So the challenge for organizations and their leaders is to create the cultural environment in which the application of worker passions and skills can be maximized. In this way, an adequate balance is created between market norm and social norm behavior in the workforce. Moving this construct from an intellectual exercise to a practical process is what we'll examine throughout this chapter, so let's take a look at a real example of this process in action.

CASE STUDY: THE DRAKE CENTER

Karen Bankston, Ph.D., is the senior vice president and head of the Drake Center, a specialized long-term acute care hospital that is located with a skilled nursing facility and an assisted living center on a 42-acre campus in Cincinnati, Ohio. Drake is part of the Health Alliance, the largest health-care system in the area. (Her leadership journey was briefly described in Chapter 1.) A strong and proactive leader, Karen has instilled the ideology at Drake that culture plays a substantive role in the success of an organization.

When Karen took on the lead role at Drake Center, the institution was viewed as an asset by the community, but it was losing $8 million to $10 million a year. If she was to stem the cash hemorrhage and get the organization to the point of at least breaking even, Karen knew that dramatic change would be necessary.

In sizing up the organization she had inherited, Karen realized that the workforce was highly skilled technically but there was a culture of apathy and oppressiveness, where the existing leaders and staff demonstrated the behaviors of individuals who had been victimized. This was an organization with no appreciation for the power of social norm thinking, where direction had been traditionally top down. Staff members were expected to follow direction without contributing to determining what that direction should be. Very little, if any, creative thinking or innovative ideas were forthcoming from employees.

These negative emotional climate conditions were problematic because increasing challenges in the health-care environment and Drake's looming financial constraints indicated that the organization's future viability would greatly depend on getting all staff members to contribute fully. Without full input and innovative thinking, Karen knew that the rapid and sustainable change necessary for Drake to continue to serve its patient population and community could not be generated, nor would she be able to transform the hospital into a widely recognized leading institution. "I believe that sustainable change requires a team of leaders who have first invested reflective time in themselves, prior to tackling the challenges that they need to face organizationally," Karen shared. So she began with this as an objective and worked to establish an environment of trust.

Karen instituted a process of direct and open communication—that is, transparency in the sharing of information—and she role-modeled the behaviors she expected from leaders and staff. As a result, the organization developed a mantra of recognizing associates as "people first, roles second," which Karen credits with "opening minds to the possibility that everyone could make a difference in the success of Drake."

The next challenge with the leadership team was to establish the importance of individual accountability so that the organization could make the journey to excellence that Karen envisioned. To do this, she adopted the "Oz Principle" as an operating platform from which to drive for results. That principle states: "One's experiences drive one's beliefs, which leads to actions, which gets results; . . . so if you want to change results, begin by changing experiences."

Karen also worked to include her staff members in structuring a new future for Drake, one in which they played a crucial role in the organization's success and were held accountable for delivering on their goals—a stark departure from the leadership expectations of past administrations. Her objective was to shift the staff mindset from that of being drones responding to hierarchical demands to that of being substantive contributors to business success. "I began to see more self-starting after this shift," Karen recalled, "but no innovation. . . . I wanted to bring out the creativity that I believed was inside these individuals, which had just not been tapped into. I told the team that this was a journey, not a sprint, and that there was so much more that could be done if we would bring our whole selves to work." Karen began searching for a process that would encourage associates to do just that.

At about this time, we began working with Karen's team members to identify their individual passion archetypes and examine the collective passions of the team. We especially focused on Drake's strategic direction and the skills and passions required for achieving aggressive business goals, while fostering the growth and utilization of knowledge within the organization. We spent a good deal of time working with individual leaders to help them internalize their passions and learn how to leverage the strengths of those passions, while minimizing the vulnerabilities. "An awakening has occurred among many members of the management team, especially the senior leaders," Karen said in a recent interview. "Individuals have shared with me that the experience [of discovering their passions and applying them to their work] has *changed their life*. Most of these individuals had not taken the time during their career to reflect on how their whole self could be used to impact their effectiveness in the workplace. They have identified that Drake is a wonderful place for them to be."

To embed this change deeply into the culture of the organization, the leadership team has now incorporated Purpose Linked Action Planning (discussed later in this chapter) into their yearly goals for personal and professional development. These plans are reviewed with Karen at least quarterly to help leaders stay the course and to determine what additional support they might need for success. "As the leader of the organization, I find staff responsiveness to this process extremely satisfying," said Karen. "This is just another step to take us to the sustainable change that is going to be required to ensure our viability into the future. What I know for sure is that culture will eat strategy for lunch—every day. So as a leader, I want to make sure that one of the major strategies we have in place is to support the culture. Identifying our major culture . . . and supporting the needs of the individuals within it, helps them to be the best that they can be—always."

The organization's hard work is paying off. In just 24 months, business results have shifted from a loss to an operating margin of $10 million, with the hospital achieving a 70 percent increase in out-of-area patient referrals and a dramatic 10-point increase in patient satisfaction scores.

Leveraging Individual and Team Passions: The Positive Performance Triad

Since most of us who were raised in a capitalist society grew up with the idea in mind that we must attend school to learn what we need to know in order to become successful at work, it's fair to say that most of us were taught to operate from a market norm perspective. We've learned that it's important to take an interest in our own skill development, which is supported, in turn, by the investment organizations make in our training. Even our early education is steeped in developing basic knowledge and skills so that we have a platform upon which to build as we progress within the educational system.

While there is no doubt that adequate skills to perform on the job are essential factors for individual success, in the normal course of obtaining a college degree, limited time and attention are devoted to the deeper exploration of our own internal workings in a way that supports the discovery of our purpose and passions. As we've noted earlier, that journey is an individual one. However, there are advantages to organizations that support the journey because skills are only one part of the equation that will lead to great performance, as we saw with the example of the Drake Center. The other critical factors to combine with employees' skills are the alignment of their passions and their values with the roles they're asked to play at work. When employees operate at the intersection of skills, passions, and values— what we call the "Performance Nexus"—they capitalize on a performance triad that provides a powerful platform for achieving results. And it's a platform that supports the market norm/social norm interplay that the organization needs within its culture.

As can be observed in Figure 14.2, if organizations focus singularly on skills, it may result in employees' doing a good job, perhaps their finding a sense of satisfaction in their work, and perhaps their being dedicated to the organization . . . at least for a while. But a focus on skills alone will also result in employees' doing just that—centering their efforts solely on applying the requisite skill to the task at hand. It does not assure that they'll look forward to determine what more might be required of them—what more might be needed to grow the business.

Skills are also a transferable commodity that workers can take to another organization, even if the one they're currently part of has financed the development of those skills. In a myopic skill-focused culture, structured primarily on market norms, the organization is exposed to a huge risk. The skills it has paid to develop in its current workforce may be the skills from which its competitors benefit when

FIGURE 14.2 POSITIVE PERFORMANCE TRIAD

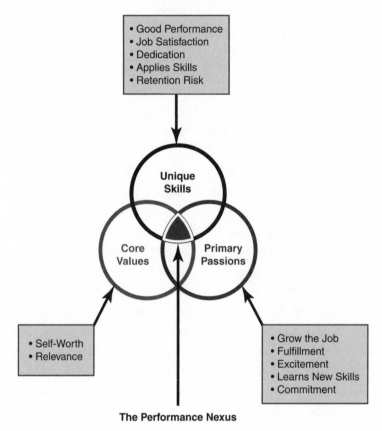

The Performance Nexus

employees are recruited away. Long term, becoming a net exporter of talent is a losing proposition for the business.

Adding passions to the mix shifts this equation. When employees utilize their skills doing work through which there is an outlet for their passions, the game changes for the organization—because the game changes for the employees. Suddenly, the individuals are not just doing a good job; they're actively growing the job. They obtain more than a sense of satisfaction *with* their work; they derive deep fulfillment *through* their daily activities, leading to a sense of excitement about their work that further enhances their commitment to the organization. When employees are operating from their passions, they do more than just apply existing skills—they willingly and actively pursue learning new skills to support the expression of those passions.

Finally, incorporating values into the triad completes the picture. Employees who are able to operate in concert with their values, within an environment where their skills and passions are aligned with their work roles, achieve a sense self-worth and relevance that further strengthens their contribution to the organization. These employees are fully engaged, difficult to recruit away, highly competent, generous with their discretionary effort, and enthusiastic about their work. The Performance Nexus—where skills, values, and passions meet—is the zone of peak performance.

Finding the Performance Nexus: Leading With Purpose

So how can leaders create a workforce where people operate from within the Performance Nexus? They can begin by applying passions— as well as skills—to how strategies are implemented, how individuals are aligned with their roles, how leaders lead others, and how the range of management systems available within the organization can support the results the organization is seeking. We call this "Leading With Purpose." The beauty of this process is that it does not require that organizations discard their management systems and adopt completely new ones. The process is additive, where new language and actions can be introduced into existing systems, enhancing the potential for those systems to generate positive results. Let's take a look at how Leading With Purpose works.

Leading With Purpose is a process for results-based leadership that examines the interface that occurs between the organization and its people through the use of management systems and tools. All large organizations and most small to midsized companies have operational systems that allow them to structure work, execute strategies, and measure the results achieved through their workforce. Leading With Purpose introduces the concept of individual passion to each of these systems and explores how it might be utilized to achieve better results.

The process begins with the foundational work that any organization must complete in order to understand what talent it wants to attract and how that talent can best be applied to growing the business. To determine these needs, organizations must begin by examining their strategies to identify the critical operational roles that will be required to execute those strategies. For these roles, organizations need to determine not only the skill set required for success in the job but also the implied passion characteristics of the role. Those characteristics are greatly dependent on the environment in which that role must function and the business situation that the incumbent in that job will face.

Next, the skills and passion archetypes of the potential incumbents for the job should be examined so that the organization can select candidates who are highly fit for the job. An ongoing practice of comparing job skills and passion characteristics to the existing talent pool of the organization helps to identify where alignment and gaps exist so that this information can be used to inform future hiring, placement, and development decisions. The important management systems and perspectives that support Leading With Purpose are these:

Recruiting, selection, and succession
Performance management and training and development
Team management and operational focus

Let's examine these in more detail.

Recruiting, Selection, and Succession

As any leader who has made a poor people decision will tell you, nothing is truer than the old adage, "Hire in haste, repent in leisure." The most critical decisions that impact the future of any organization occur when a choice is being made to bring a new person into the organization, whether from the outside or through an internal placement.

Much is invested in identifying the right talent for a job: countless hours are devoted to developing job descriptions, creating employment ads, screening résumés, checking references, and interviewing candidates. The whole process can take an extended time period to complete, and it can require an investment of significant amounts of money—and how disheartening and costly it is, for both the organization and the employee, when things don't work out as planned.

While conducting our initial study on purpose and passion, we asked participants if anyone ever asked them to articulate their purpose or share their passions during an interview process, or at any other time during their careers. Want to guess how many said yes? If you guessed zero, you win the prize. That's right. No leader and no hiring manager had ever asked these participants the most fundamental of questions—the one that might tell them a great deal about who that person was and how they might best contribute to the organization. True, they'd been asked about their background and experience, technical skills, and education—some were even asked about their golf handicap and favorite operas. But none of them were asked about what truly drives them. So the one change that could be made to the way individuals are recruited is so simple that we hesitate to mention it here, but we do so because it is so often overlooked. Organizations should include inquiry into candidate passions as a standard part of the interview process. It's not tough to do because it requires adding to the interview list just a few simple questions such as these:

- What are you most passionate about and why?
- How do you envision applying those passions in this job or with our organization?
- How are you applying those passions now?

Imagine the interesting discussion that these questions might elicit, a discussion that would provide deep insight into the content of the candidates' character. The candidates' responses might even provide evidence of how their values impact their actions and how their skills have been developed to support their passions.

Once a hiring decision is made, assessing a new hire's passion archetypes can provide important information that can be utilized to quickly integrate the person into the organization. Imagine how much a leader can learn about a new employee through a discussion about his or her deep core drivers. A leader's early understanding of a new hire's passions can allow that leader to make better decisions about that individual's job assignments and ongoing development, significantly reducing the time required for full onboarding of a new employee.

A New Recruiting Tool: A Pair of Sneakers

In one organization we've worked with, we found a leader who was legendary for his interview process. This individual, we'll call him "David," was a vice president with a large manufacturing multinational, and his perspective on the hiring process was anything but traditional and was far outside the confines of the standard practices of his company.

The organization had a well-defined interview procedure that included a targeted selection process in which each interviewer would be assigned a particular area to review with the candidate. All interviewers had been trained in this process and in effective interviewing techniques. The interview team would meet at the end of the day (what they called a "Huddle") to share their findings and decide the fate of each candidate. David would choose not to follow the standard interview practice, yet he repeatedly uncovered the most interesting and meaningful information about each candidate, which never failed to inform the team's decision during Huddle. What was his secret weapon? A pair of sneakers.

David's view of the world was this: "By the time I see the candidates, their skills and educational background have already been vetted. What I most want to learn is what makes them tick as people. What are they excited about? What makes them angry? How are they going to bring all that they are to the work of this company? How will they respond to change?" When candidates came to David's office prepared for yet another traditional interview, they were in for a big surprise. He'd greet them at the door in his sneakers, offer to let them leave their personal belongings in his office, and then escort them on a hike through the wooded property surrounding the office complex. It didn't matter what the weather was like, or how well dressed the candidates were, David might spend one to three hours with them, walking and learning about who they are. His inquiries led candidates to a level of introspection about themselves that exceeded any other interview process they'd experienced. For some, that introspection helped them to understand that the job or the organization was not the best fit for them. For others, it helped to clarify that among all the organizations they might be considering, David's was the one in which they'd be able make the greatest impact.

To this day, individuals who were hired through his process describe the interview with David as the most meaningful they've ever experienced. The organization significantly improved its results through this process as well, with a large percentage of the candidates hired through this process going on to achieve great success with the company.

Escaping a Succession Disaster

Succession decisions present a similar opportunity for capitalizing on the power of the passions of individual candidates. Consider for a moment the process that many organizations use for succession planning. It's designed to identify the high-potential talent in the organization—say, the top 5 percent of performers in the company. In most cases, these individuals are listed in the succession plan in accordance with their "readiness" to move to a designated higher position, one normally selected based on their acquired skills and experiences. Nowhere in the process does the average organization examine the passions of their high potentials or explore how those passions might be pivotal in their success as they move up the ladder.

We've worked with one organization in which examining the passions of their leading candidates for a senior position became quite essential. This U.S.-based manufacturer had been struggling for some time with eroding market share. The company's plan for dealing with this issue included, among other things, developing a global marketing strategy that would be implemented in countries around the world. Prior to this time, individuals within the countries had controlled their own marketing strategies, and the results had been uneven—at best.

When we examined the job description for the leader of this new global marketing function, we found that the position would be headquartered in North Carolina, but it would require extensive interaction with international markets. As we saw it, the person best suited for the job of executive vice president for global marketing would of course need the requisite skills but would also need to be a passionate Connector/Transformer if he or she were to achieve the level of cooperation needed from marketing teams in various countries. When we examined the core challenges of the job, it was clear that this leader would need to work well with a variety of cultures and would face a great deal of resistance to change as he or she tried to centralize marketing. The marketing staffs in a number of countries had been operating for years in relative isolation, with freedom from oversight by headquarters. The company president believed that the marketing staffs in these countries were unlikely to give up autonomy without a fight.

The HR director presented the background on the two leading succession plan candidates, "Jeremy" and "Raj," both of whom had enjoyed stellar careers with the company. Both candidates were in their early forties, had been in their jobs about the same amount of time, and had similar two-year performance ratings. Jeremy had been based in the United States most of his career, with some experience working in Canada. As VP of U.S. marketing, he was viewed internally as a marketing genius, and he had worked closely with a consulting firm hired by his company to develop some cutting-edge marketing tools. From a passion perspective, Jeremy was a strong Conceiver/Processor—a great idea guy with a passion for structure and analysis.

The second candidate, Raj, was born in India, and he had worked internationally throughout his career. He spent three years in a U.S. headquarters position in which he excelled, before being assigned to head marketing for Scandinavia. Raj demonstrated excellent marketing skills, but he also excelled in developing high-performing teams.

Through the efforts of his team, the marketing function in Scandinavia was transformed to become one of the most competitive in the industry. His primary passions were Connector/Transformer—someone who flourishes in building relationships and orchestrating change, while helping others to embrace it.

During our initial discussions, the HR head felt strongly that Jeremy was the right candidate for the EVP global marketing position. After all, he had deep U.S. roots, knew everyone at headquarters, and was one of the brightest marketing guys in the industry. What hadn't been considered was what Jeremy was actually passionate about doing. In our discussions with him, it was clear that he most enjoyed the deep conceptual thinking required in his current project with the outside consultant. While he was skilled to perform many aspects of marketing, he was less excited about dealing with people issues or with negotiations, both of which would be essential in the EVP position. The more we talked, the more this situation was looking a lot like the one with James, the ill-fitting country manager for Hong Kong described in this book's introduction.

To our delight, this story, which could have resulted in a major loss of talent for the company, had a pleasant outcome. The HR head and the person to whom the EVP position reported sat down with the candidates individually to learn more about them and discuss their passions. It became clear from these discussions that Jeremy didn't see himself as the best fit for the EVP position and he wanted instead to focus his career in the area of strategy. Raj, on the other hand, would enjoy implementing the new marketing strategy and working across cultures, but he would be less excited about spending his time developing global strategies. With two outstanding candidates in the pipeline, the company did not want to lose either in the process of this succession decision. Instead, based on these discussions, they chose to reexamine the job and created two senior positions, one that would focus on broad implementation of the global strategy and the other that would focus on strategic analysis and future planning. In this way, both Raj and Jeremy were able to continue to contribute to the organization's success.

Performance Management and Training and Development

One of the most important discussions that employees have with their leaders relates to the goals they commit to and the results they actually produce. However, these discussions also provide a prime opportunity to explore individual passions and determine ways to apply them to successfully achieving the objectives for which the employees are held accountable. Depending on the organization, the process of setting objectives and managing for optimal performance can be an elaborate exercise in which goals established at the top of the pyramid trickle down through various levels in the organization, with employees in each subsequent level of the hierarchy defining the portion of the overall objectives they will commit to delivering. This process has a variety of labels; some organizations call it "management by objectives" (MBO); 3M India calls it the "Contribution and Development Summary"; and GE used to call it "Working, Planning, and Review."

In organizations that wish to fully optimize the advantages of the Performance Nexus described earlier, careful consideration needs to be applied to performance management and employee training and development. To begin, let's examine changes to the goal setting process that is part of most performance management systems.

We recommend that an "individual fulfillment" goal be established and measured much like the other objectives to which the employees and their managers are held accountable. For this goal, the employees would define how they will apply their passions to their role at work, be it through a particular project or as part of their ongoing daily activities. They would also measure their progress toward this goal at the end of the plan period. In other words, they'd identify the actions they took to apply their passions to a particular activity and assess the impact of doing so (for example, project results, their own level of engagement in the work, or new ideas generated). This approach results in three useful outcomes for the organization and the individuals:

1. *It encourages the kind of deep introspection in the employees that supports increased self-knowledge—a critical attribute of developing leaders.*

2. *The employees and their leaders will be able to see the direct connection between individual passions and work assignments, pointing to the potential that exists for applying those passions to obtaining great results and gaining fulfillment at work.*

3. *It supports development planning, so that leaders and employees can more accurately identify the kind of training and on-the-job experiences that are most likely to be enhanced by the employees' passions, thus supporting their learning uptake.*

This last point is an important one. Consider how much money organizations invest in training their workforce, and think of the multitude of training programs that you've probably attended during your career. How many of them truly changed you? We suspect that the ones you most benefited from allowed you to develop a side of yourself that supported your passions, be they programs designed to build technical skills or training courses to make you a better leader. Doesn't it just make good sense to align training with individual passions whenever possible? Passion is what makes learning stick, so the organization receives the greatest return on investment when passion is factored into employee development decisions.

When we work with leaders to create high-performing teams, we focus heavily on development planning that is tailored to each individual. The planning is firmly rooted in the skill needs of the organization, as well as the passion drivers of the individual. For this reason, in addition to leaders' creating a traditional employee development plan that may vary in format from organization to organization, we recommend that all team members complete a *Purpose Linked Action Plan* that focuses on how they will apply their passions to both organizational and personal objectives. It complements the traditional development plan, which typically identifies required skill building and experiential learning needs.

In focusing on purpose and passions as an action planning exercise, individuals are encouraged to examine their guiding professional and personal values and find where those intersect with the operating values of the organization. They are also required to develop a *statement of purpose*, which defines who they are beyond their work roles or relationships with others. When this activity is completed, employees identify their guiding passions and the actions they intend to take to apply those passions in their work and personal life. To make the action plan manageable, we suggest that employees identify two to three professional and personal objectives that they plan to achieve, taking care to assign deadlines for those objectives and identify the resources they'll need and actions they must take to achieve them.

Through this more comprehensive development planning, we encourage employees to structure their objectives in manageable six-month blocks and limit their focus to two to three goals at a time. By defining milestones that will allow them to measure their success, individuals can connect their accomplishments more directly to the internal purpose that drives the passions they exhibit. As one client shared with us, "I am a little 'tough nut'—not easily cracked, but I honestly followed the invite into a deeper understanding of myself, hoping that I could either confirm my current direction or alter it to find a more fulfilling experience. It was slightly more difficult than most 'homework' assignments, but the yield was well worth it. While the concept is a simple one—that in order to be productive, one must be simply happy and satisfied—the work that needs to be completed in order to find this truth is much tougher, but certainly worth the sweat equity."

Teams, Passions, and the Knowledge Factor

Imagine that you are the head of global business development for a leading IT firm, and you have determined that expanding into India is a major plank in your platform for success. You further decide that making this expansion a reality will require a robust workforce, with cutting-edge technology skills that will allow your company to outperform its rivals in this very competitive industry, where ongoing knowledge acquisition is crucial for survival. A major tactical objective that you define is to enhance the skill training of engineers coming out of the Indian educational system, with the intention of hiring these engineers into your company. This is exactly the challenge Cisco Systems is facing, as leaders work to develop local knowledge infrastructures in this very important geographic region. They are structuring a Global Talent Acceleration Program in Bangalore, India. So what passions might be essential to have on the team charged with this challenging objective?

Understanding the myriad ways in which the organization might capitalize on the talent and technology interface possible in the region would be greatly supported by a team composed of Builders, Connectors, Conceivers, and Teachers. The Builders on the team would be most passionate about creating a platform for business in the region. They'll work diligently, in partnership with Connectors, to structure deals with local universities and acquire facilities to host the training programs, and they will work to build the infrastructure required to orchestrate the objective. The Connectors will help build relationships with local thought leaders who can assist in recruiting talent to the program. The Conceivers on the team would be excited about generating new ideas and approaches to developing the very best talent, and they would identify new ways in which that talent might be utilized. The Teachers on the team would be instrumental in mentoring and education, providing a robust curriculum to transfer knowledge quickly.

While the Cisco example points to four critical passions for team success, in reality all of the archetypes of passion are essential if knowledge is to be created and utilized in a way that supports business growth. Ultimately, organizations have three major levers for business success:

- They can leverage what they have: money, resources, and people.
- They can leverage what they do: produce products and offer services.
- And they can leverage what they know: the institutional learning and knowledge within the organization.

One of the most valuable assets of any business is its ability to develop and utilize knowledge. This is true for Cisco, and it is true for your team as well. The passion archetypes play a powerful role in this process because they can be described by how they contribute to the generation and flow of organizational knowledge. We call their collective impact the "Passion Driven Knowledge Cycle," as seen in Figure 14.3.

Figure 14.3 Passion Driven Knowledge Cycle

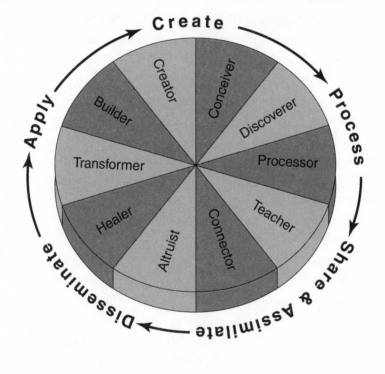

In this cycle there are five modes of influence that the archetypes can have on knowledge:

Archetypes may create knowledge by generating new concepts and new ideas.

Archetypes may process knowledge for individuals or groups so that the knowledge can be interpreted in meaningful ways.

Archetypes may share and assimilate knowledge so that others can learn from it.

Archetypes may disseminate knowledge or the products of knowledge so that others can benefit from it.

Finally, archetypes may apply knowledge in ways that support the growth of the organization and the expansion of the business.

It is important to note that gaps in the composition of archetypes on a team or in an organization can significantly impact the flow of knowledge and the benefits that could be derived from an intact knowledge cycle.

Team Management and Operational Focus

As we consider the impact of passion on how teams perform, the distinct operational perspectives of the archetypes become meaningful. What the operational focus of the archetypes helps to delineate is where each individual can best contribute to the team from a passion perspective. It also helps to clarify how individual team members interact and how erroneous perceptions of behavior can be developed that are actually a reflection of one's passions.

For example, we once worked with a team that had a high proportion of Builders and Transformers, a few Teachers, and one lone Processor. The Builders and Transformers were working splendidly together to create a new business division in Singapore. The Teachers were very effective in defining the development needs of the newly hired staff and worked well with the Builders and Transformers on the team. The lone Processor was struggling for a seat at the table, often finding his voice drowned out by others on the team. From the Processor's perspective, the team was on the right track with building a new division, but it had failed to realize that there were funding constraints and governmental regulations that might delay the timeline they planned to establish for completing the project. Worse yet, he knew they were all going to be measured against the deadline they were planning to set.

While working with the team, it became apparent to us that the Processor of the group was being marginalized because he was viewed as a deterrent to progress. In his effort to get the team to slow down long enough to consider the complications he saw on the horizon, he had been unfairly labeled as the just-say-no finance guy who pinched every penny as if it were his personal money. In reality, he wanted the division to be successful, and he was working to create structure and systems that he felt were essential for operations. In working with this group to define their passion archetypes, their views on the Processor shifted, as the team gained new understanding about the operational perspectives that this archetype carries. The operational focus of each archetype is highlighted in Figure 14.4.

As the members of the Singapore leadership team began to understand each other more completely, they came to realize that their

FIGURE 14.4 PRIMARY OPERATIONAL PERSPECTIVES OF EACH ARCHETYPE

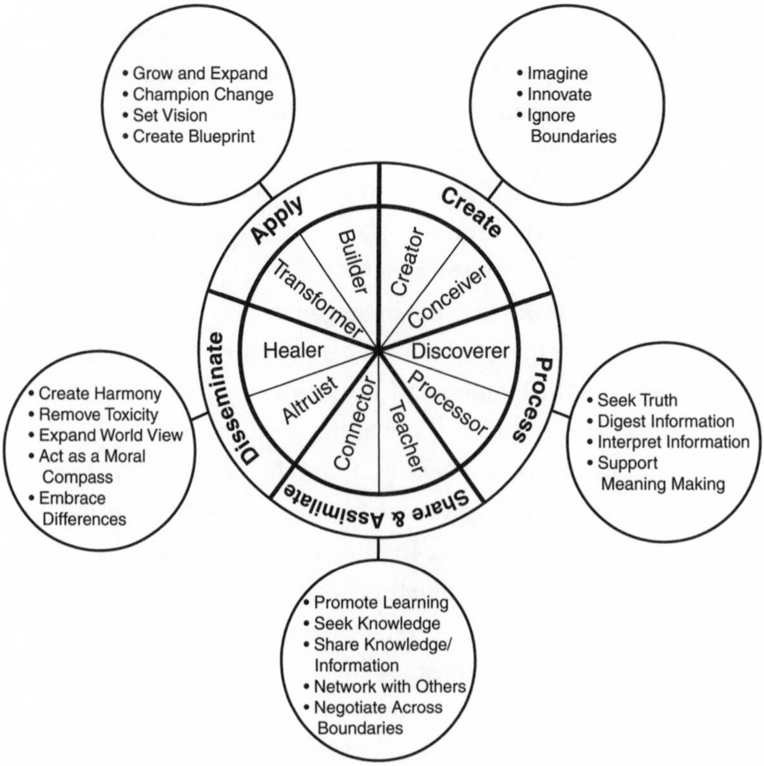

Processor had the best interests of the business at heart. He was excellent at digesting and interpreting the financial and governmental information on which the team members relied to execute their strategy. Ultimately, the team's Processor was able to create the financial systems that allowed the team to make meaning of what was happening in the marketplace, so that they could set realistic goals and garner the resources to achieve them.

This team example provides an important lesson for leaders about the value of having multiple archetypes on a team. The passion archetypes present a new form of diversity in a language that can be understood by all, regardless of race, gender, or background. The barriers to understanding that once existed collapse with the knowledge of how each respective archetype contributes to the team. That's a powerful lever for success.

Today's business leaders are actively mining for the new ideas and perspectives that operating from a platform of team passions can provide. While plumbing for diverse viewpoints—even the dissenting viewpoints—and edge-shifting concepts, passionate leaders understand that it's inadvisable to be satisfied with only sanitized and safe recommendations. Following that safe advice may render a business future that's anything but secure. Instead, these teams and their leaders examine not only the decisions they have made but also the challenges they experienced in making them. Leaders of teams that are powered by passion will always ask, "What are the good ideas that the team has left on the table untouched, and how can we use them to produce creative new results?"

 FIFTEEN

How Great Leaders Leverage Passion

THE TASK OF LEADERSHIP IS NOT TO PUT GREATNESS INTO HUMANITY,
BUT TO ELICIT IT, FOR THE GREATNESS IS ALREADY THERE.
—JOHN BUCHAN

In the latter months of 2008, businesses around the globe faced an economic crisis that would prove to test the mettle of many organizational leaders. Reading the front page of the *Wall Street Journal* was disturbingly similar to reading the obituaries, except we were learning about the plight of once seemingly invincible companies. Consider these headlines over a three-day period in November:

Citigroup plans to cut at least 10,000 more jobs and will raise interest rates on credit card customers.[1]

U.S. Steel will lay off 675 union workers due to slackening demand for steel products.[2]

Most of Europe officially fell into recession . . .[3]

Freddie Mac posted a $25.3 billion loss and said it will need a $13.8 billion cash infusion.[4]

Fidelity detailed a second round of layoffs that will bring total job cuts to about 3,000.[5]

Sun Microsystems will cut up to 6,000 jobs to cope with a high-tech spending slowdown.[6]

Nokia issued a profit warning, saying its core devices and services business will be hit as consumers curtail spending.[7]

GM blitzes Washington in a bid for aid.[8]

In a climate in which many businesses are in a fight for survival, leaders will be called upon to lead as never before. The future of their organizations will depend in large part on their ability to engage the whittled-down and battle-worn workforce in a way that gets people believing that there is still something worth fighting for, some important way in which they can shape a better future for the organization and for themselves. We're in an age of both reason and meaning, when leading from the head and the heart will be essential—a clarion call for bringing the whole of who we are to work, because anything less is simply not enough.

The leaders of purpose linked organizations, when confronting challenging times, will not ask, "How will we succeed?" Instead they'll ask, "Why will we succeed?" In asking the how question, these leaders understand that they are likely to address only the tactics that might be applied to growing the business and navigating in changing times. It is the why question that gets at the heart—the purpose and passions that drive individual behaviors and motivate employees to deliver results. If these leaders have taken responsibility for creating a culture in which employee purpose and passion can flourish in partnership with skills and values, they'll be able to say that their formula for success is anchored in the following facts:

- The individual purpose of our people is aligned with the mission of our organization.
- The passions and skills of our people are aligned with the roles we ask them to play and with organizational goals.
- Our people value what our organization values.
- Our leaders embody their passions and bring them to bear on our toughest business challenges; they help others to do the same.
- Our collective passions help us to learn—from both our failures and our victories.
- Our culture operates with a worldview of abundance rather than scarcity, so we celebrate often and lament rarely.

What is certain in these changing times is the need for organizations to arrive at creative solutions; passion is what arouses the curiosity and imagination required to deliver those solutions. It's the primordial soup from which innovation is born. In an economic environment where no company can afford to waste resources, tapping into the discretionary effort that passion stimulates leads to revitalized growth through inventive ideas.

Leaders who are themselves truly passionate ignite the kind of passion-based performance in others that is so crucial in challenging times. Researchers have called these leaders "transformational" because through their passion, they are able to give meaning to work and help others find purpose in their work that extends beyond the nature of the task itself.[9] So who are these leaders, and how do they inspire winning teams to get great results? Are they the engaging and charismatic individuals that we read about, with attractive physical features and flashy personalities—or are they different? And just what is charisma anyway?

If you check the dictionary, you'll find that it is defined as "a special magnetic charm or appeal" and it is derived from the Greek word *charisma*, meaning "favor" or "gift." However, a number of researchers believe that some apparently charismatic leaders do not actually achieve the best long-term results for their organizations. In the now classic leadership book *Good to Great*, for example, Jim Collins points out that charisma may actually be a handicap because it may compel the workforce to focus more on the leader than on the realities of the business.[10] In fact, he found that some of the best leaders in companies producing outstanding results were actually quite humble personalities.

We're not going to engage in the debate about the relative value of charismatic leaders, but we would like to offer another perspective. We believe that great leaders could best be described as *inspirational* rather than charismatic because they lead from a center of purpose and passion. The focus of the inspirational leader is developing other leaders rather than gathering additional followers—as a result, they build winning teams. These leaders know themselves well and intimately understand the members of their teams—they make others feel relevant rather than anonymous. Ultimately, they mirror the humility that Collins observed in great leaders because they are authentic and approachable.

Interestingly, there is no magic in the way these leaders operate. No smoke, no mirrors, no requisite eloquent presentations. Instead, they do one thing particularly well. They give employees a role to play that's consistent with their Performance Nexus—so they constantly leverage the unique skills, core values, and primary passions of everyone in the workforce. In Collins's words, they focus on "getting the right people on the bus, in the right seat." When inspirational leaders make hiring decisions, they think individually instead of being myopically focused on a fixed position. Thus they bring in the best people and assign them to the seats determined by the nature of the jobs that are most resonant with the employees' skills, passions, and values. In short, inspirational leaders help others to determine what they can be best at and then create that opportunity for them inside the organization.

Over the years, we've observed that leaders generally operate on a continuum somewhere between inspirational and cynical. The best leaders work diligently to ward off the cynicism and fear that business exigencies can engender and stay centered on the purpose that fuels their passions. Inspirational leaders look for ways to focus on the opportunities while managing the dangers that business challenges present, and they help others in the organization to do the same. Through passion, they view the world as abundant in opportunity, and when challenged by a crisis, they recognize, as Nobel laureate chemist Ilya Prigogine discovered, that a new order will always emerge from chaos. Inspirational leaders are better at identifying an emerging new order because their connection to their purpose and passions compels them to look for the possibilities cloaked within the chaos of the business environment. Confident about the promise of the future, they don't hesitate to initiate the transformational changes in the organization that a new order might dictate.

We invite you to examine the Inspiration Continuum in Figure 15.1 and rate yourself as a leader on the following scale. As you work to move on the continuum toward inspirational leadership and engage the workforce in a way that generates great results, some important questions to ask yourself are these:

- Do I understand my own passions?
- Do I understand the passions of the people working for and with me?
- Do I do everything that I can to make the people I work with feel relevant to the organization and its purpose?
- Do I take time to deeply understand the concerns, needs, and sources of joy in the people I work with?
- Do I do everything that I can do to reward them—not only by compensating them fairly but also by giving them roles or assignments that they will find fulfilling?
- Do I understand what new knowledge, experience, or skills my people have gained since joining the company that I'm not making the most of in the way I ask them to work?
- Do I seek input from my people to shape the work environment as aggressively as I seek customer input to shape our products or services?
- Does their success matter to me as much or more than my own?

FIGURE 15.1 INSPIRATION CONTINUUM

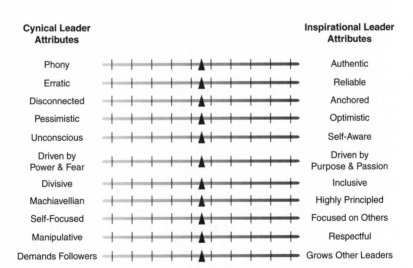

Cynical Leader Attributes		Inspirational Leader Attributes
Phony		Authentic
Erratic		Reliable
Disconnected		Anchored
Pessimistic		Optimistic
Unconscious		Self-Aware
Driven by Power & Fear		Driven by Purpose & Passion
Divisive		Inclusive
Machiavellian		Highly Principled
Self-Focused		Focused on Others
Manipulative		Respectful
Demands Followers		Grows Other Leaders

In purpose linked organizations, the job of the inspirational leader is to provide employees with the license to thrive. Great leaders accomplish this by demonstrating a genuine interest in their people and a desire to know them at a deeper level. By connecting others' work to a larger purpose, these leaders help individuals on their team feel valued and relevant, and they create adequate interplay between market norm and social norm thinking in the culture. Doing so generates the kind of energy that can be harnessed to achieve results so that people become propelled by their own engines. Instead of struggling to push others toward a goal, inspirational leaders unleash the employee passions that are needed to catapult the organization to greatness.

Engaging the Whole to Get Results

We spoke with two leaders whose inspirational styles particularly impressed us. Both leaders have shaped their companies' focus on engaging the heads and hearts of employees, which helps them harness the energy it creates to achieve sustainable business results. These leaders operate in very different business sectors, and their companies have different organizational architectures. One leader is operating a privately held U.S.-based company, and the other, based in Switzerland, leads a public firm whose products are household staples. What's unusual about these two individuals is their unwavering application of the formulas for igniting employee passions that they have embedded into the culture of their organizations. Through their example, these inspirational leaders demonstrate what a powerful role a consistent focus on purpose and passion plays in both achieving great financial results and in harnessing the ongoing commitment of the workforce.

The first of these leaders is Marilyn Carlson Nelson, the chair of Carlson, a privately held group of global companies operating in 150 countries. Carlson provides hotel, restaurant, travel, and marketing services, and it includes brands such as Radisson Hotels, Park Plaza, Park Inn, Country Inn and Suites, Regent hotels and resorts, Carlson Wagonlit Travel, Carlson Marketing, and T.G.I. Friday's restaurants.

As the head of an organization employing 160,000 people world-wide, Marilyn deeply understands the value of engagement and continually searches for ways to create a fun and rewarding environment in which people are encouraged to contribute their best. She inherited the organization from her father, whom Marilyn described as "a command and control leader who had difficulty engaging the two generations below him." The company's culture suffered as a result. But since her tenure at the helm, the organization has almost doubled its revenue base to nearly $40 billion, and it has vastly increased its representation of women at the top.

Carlson utilizes a leadership model which has self-leadership as a core around which discipline, stewardship, relationship building, and performance satellite. Through it, Marilyn continually seeks out leaders who are competitive and performance oriented but at the same time are good stewards of the business who won't sell out the future for a short-term gain. Marilyn says that Carlson looks for leaders "who can connect the dots and work across sectors." But these leaders need to care as much about others' success as they do about their own.

To achieve a fully engaged and passionate workforce, Carlson has implemented a scorecard system, whereby employees are surveyed for feedback on the climate in their department and the impact of their supervisor. The company has proven that the units with the best scores—the ones that are most engaged—produce the best business results.

Marilyn's Altruist passion has drawn her to examine the succession planning process at Carlson and seek more inclusiveness in the organization. "I graduated from college at a time when women were not given opportunities," she shared. "I promised myself that as I had the chance to create change, I would use it to create a meritocracy." She believes that her drive to draw from the whole labor pool has shaped Carlson's culture for the better and increased its competitiveness. When the company found that its succession process resulted in women and minorities making it to the list of top talent but rarely being selected for senior-level promotions, Marilyn decided it was a system that needed changing. Consequently, the company began to conduct 360-degree assessments with their high-potential talent pool to identify developmental needs earlier so that needed skills could be obtained before promotional opportunities became available. As a result, women now comprise nearly 40 percent of the executive ranks at Carlson.

Even when her positions have been controversial, Marilyn has continued to live by her passions and convictions. An avid philanthropist, she has instituted giving as an integral part of the culture at Carlson, and she insists that "it is not just a marketing tool." Carlson is a founder of the World Childhood Foundation, which has focused efforts on homeless children around the world. Through her association with this organization, Marilyn was asked by the U.S. Department of State to support an effort to protect the more than 1 million children around the globe who are victims of sexual trafficking. Under her leadership, Carlson took a stand and made it publicly known that the company would not do business with traffickers or permit any child prostitution in its hotels. In fact, Carlson was the first global U.S. company in the industry to sign a code of conduct to end child prostitution and trafficking. Marilyn continues to encourage other firms to follow suit. "It's a dark subject," she said, "but we feel [that dealing with it openly] is consistent with who we are. We're going to keep ringing the bell and raising the alarm on this. It's the only way to protect our own children."

Even a purpose linked organization like Carlson is not immune to a downturn in the economy. Marilyn believes that communicating from the heart with employees is crucial in tough times, but she warns other leaders that the job is much harder if you haven't been communicating all along. It's a time when her Connector and Healer passions make a difference. "I tell our people that we've been in this business over 70 years—through the Great Depression, World War II, oil shortages, the Gulf War, and so on. While it's our desire to keep everyone employed, the reality is that we may need to downsize to stay competitive and protect the greatest possible number of jobs. As things grow again, people will hopefully come back." She believes that if you communicate honestly in good times, it helps you in tough times because employees "see your honest intentions."

In her book *How We Lead Matters*, Marilyn highlights many of the leadership insights she has gathered from guiding the organization through challenging times in the past. She believes the future will hold more difficult choices for everyone. Carlson employees, for example, know that with cutbacks they may have to step into leadership roles and take on additional responsibility that they didn't expect, but they also know that executives will not profit personally from job reductions. "If [employees] see leaders making a sacrifice," said Marilyn, "they'll [work hard to] surpass anything you could ever imagine." Perhaps the best reflection of Carlson's appreciation for the whole each employee brings to work is captured in the company credo that defines Marilyn's leadership:

> Whatever you do, do with Integrity.
> Wherever you go, go as a Leader.
> Whomever you serve, serve with Caring.
> Whenever you dream, dream with your All.
> And never, ever give up.

A Human Company

Peter Brabeck-Letmathe is an inspirational leader who is the chairman of Nestlé, a leading nutrition, health, and wellness company with sales in excess of 107.6 billion Swiss francs (roughly $88.6 billion). Nestlé is known worldwide for many popular household brands such as Nescafé coffee, Häagen-Dazs ice cream, and Gerber baby foods, as well as nutritional products, prepared foods, pet foods, and beverages. With its stake of close to 52 percent in Alcon and its joint venture with L'Oréal, it also has a presence in the pharmaceutical and cosmetic markets.

Over the 12-year period ending in December 2007, Nestlé provided its shareholders with a total return of 408 percent, and it has delivered improved top-line and bottom-line growth each year. Even in 2008, when many companies reported significant losses as the global economic environment deteriorated, Nestlé delivered a 2.2 percent growth in sales over the prior year and an organic growth of

8.3 percent. It is a complex, decentralized organization that operates in a multitude of countries and cultures around the world through which it has delivered these impressive results. The primary mechanism through which Nestlé has leveraged the purpose and passions of its employees to achieve these gains is by creating a culture of dedicated adherence to important leadership and management principles, within an operating framework that focuses on long-term sustainability.

At first glance, the Nestlé culture would seem to be strictly revenue focused, but a conversation with Peter Brabeck-Letmathe will quickly expand that view. "Without a doubt, I believe that passionate employee commitment and alignment with company roles are extremely important," he shared. "The day that I became CEO, we published the Nestlé Management and Leadership Principles"—the company bible for leadership beliefs and behaviors to which every Nestlé leader is held accountable. These principles are the foundation from which the organization leverages the passions of its workforce.

What is striking about the company document is that it begins this way: "Nestlé is a human company providing a response to individual human needs throughout the world with specific concern for the well-being of both its consumers and employees. This is reflected in its attitude and its sense of responsibility toward people. Nestlé aims to increase sales and profits, but at the same time to raise the standard of living everywhere it is active and the quality of life for everyone."[11]

The statement is powerful and intentionally emotional, and it invites leaders to engage with their teams in the business of the organization using this framework as a guideline. It also challenges them to deeply examine their own passions and values for alignment with the principles. It's a challenge that Peter has accepted, as he reflected on his purpose and passions and their influence on his own leadership. "Everything that I am has shaped my approach to this company," he said. "Raising the standard of living wherever we operate is not a single-minded economic objective. We want to achieve success, but in service to others—and we want our people to feel that they belong to something that is greater than themselves." As we have demonstrated in earlier chapters of this book, the value of this objective is well documented by research, which proves that doing work that is infused with meaning is a central factor in employee performance and well-being.

The Nestlé leadership principles—which include commitment to quality, respect for other cultures and traditions, and values such as trust, mutual respect, tolerance, pragmatism, and curiosity—have guided the company's selection and advancement of leaders. Passion and a willingness to apply the principles are the key criteria for hiring and promotion throughout the organization. "You can be the best in your field and not make it here," said Peter. "During an interview, I discuss the leadership principles before everything else. If I get the feeling that the person can't identify with these, then I know it won't work. We hire first for character and then for the rest."

The leadership principles also serve as a valuable compass in this largely decentralized organization, where every leader is expected to espouse them through action. The principles provide a consistent internal cultural thread that is woven throughout Nestlé facilities around the world, regardless of differences in local culture and custom. The thread is further reinforced by members of the company's executive board, who spend a great deal of time in the field communicating with the workforce. Peter himself spends 28 days each year in the International Training Center in Switzerland communicating and reinforcing the leadership principles. He engages employees in conversation about how the principles should impact their actions, and he spends time in every market. "I'm constantly talking about the principles and asking questions," Peter shared. "In a decentralized organization, communication is critical."

A corporate governance philosophy that is focused on the long term has been the other key to Nestlé's success. Peter believes that a culture that resists succumbing to short-term financial pressures will not compromise the future sustainability of the business. Likewise, with a long-term focus, there is continuity in leadership thinking and sustained application of employee passions to the objectives of the organization. As a result, leaders develop greater credibility with their teams because they are able to implement plans and see them through to fruition, rather than engaging in the frenzy of quarter-to-quarter management, which so often results in good plans being scraped midstream.

This form of governance has become even more essential for prospering in a difficult economic environment. Peter expected Nestlé's results in 2008 to be better than all previous years, and he maintains his confidence about 2009. "We do not have an atmosphere of panic in the organization. We believe our operating model can help us to overcome economic challenges. . . . We have a deep pipeline, and though we'll adjust sales growth targets downward somewhat, we will continue to move forward nonetheless. The most important thing our principles have helped us to do is to create leadership credibility."

In today's stormy economic times, those principles have served Nestlé well. The company's steady organic growth and long-term focus may well position it to increase market share as other competitors succumb to the pressures of a depressed market. Their ability to retain and motivate a workforce through the leadership principles has complemented Nestlé's governance philosophy, and it has promoted a cultural belief that succeeding with others is more motivating than succeeding alone. What Peter's passionate leadership has created for nearly 276,000 Nestlé employees around the globe is more a lifestyle than a job.

Permission to Be

Throughout our years of working with leaders around the globe, we have operated with one basic philosophy—that most individuals who find themselves in leadership roles innately want to succeed at bringing out the best in their people. Yes, we've met the occasional egomaniac and self-centered, miscast, greedy, or cynical executive, but by and large, most of the leaders we've met are committed to making a positive difference in the work lives of their teams. These leaders are hungry for tools that can assist them with accomplishing the essential objective of growing talent for the organization.

Until recently, much of the focus on people development concentrated on building or enhancing skills and providing experiences through which someone could learn. However, it's not enough anymore to possess only the skills for a job. The volatility of the business environment now demands agility and a robust perception that skills alone cannot provide. The kind of awareness and knowledge building that evolve from the effective application of the collective passions of the organization are what will distinguish a company from its competitors.

In recent years, two momentous changes have occurred that will require organizations to adopt a new platform for people development. First, there has been a shift in employee expectations related to the degree of personal fulfillment they expect to obtain through their work. Second, there are cataclysmic changes in the economy that have driven organizations to reexamine the framework for their survival and future prosperity. Consider for a moment the shortcomings of the era from which the business world is emerging:

- We've witnessed greed drive the collapse of the banking system in the United States and abroad.
- Customers' and employees' distrust of companies is increasing.
- There is growing realization that government alone cannot repair the damaged economic environment.
- Lowered customer expectations about the buying experience are leading to customers' decreased loyalties to brands and companies.
- The pride and sense of belonging that employees previously enjoyed with their organizations is eroding, which is impacting productivity and the personal satisfaction so critical to individual well-being.

While these changes have occurred in the last two decades, additional shifts of even larger proportion have occurred over the last century in the cultural environment. The world has moved from the Industrial Revolution to the postindustrial society, characterized by the Information Age and a Web-wired world. However, today's changes in the economy and in employee needs are calling forth yet another evolution of the business environment. We have now entered the Era of Consciousness.

In this new era, leaders will be called upon to become profoundly aware of themselves and their teams, to help those they lead discover and apply their passions to the work of the organization, to become deeply aware of the customers they serve and the value that company products and services can offer, and to understand intimately the diversity of the cultures and countries in which their organizations operate. The organizations in which these leaders function must morph and grow in response to the flatter world environment, or they will suffer the fate of all living systems that are unable to adapt and transition in the face of change.

There is so much to be accomplished in organizations operating in this new era that it behooves leaders to make the best and most efficient use of their people. Can employees be counted on to care about all of the issues on the company radar scope? Probably not. But they will care deeply and passionately about those issues that can be traced back to the heart of who they are. By providing individuals with permission to be all that they are and to apply who they are to their work roles, inspirational leaders can forge the essential connection between employees and the living system that is the organization. In turn, this will allow individuals and organizations to discover a new way forward together—where operating from the zone of employee purpose and passion is a matter of design rather than a matter of chance.

ACKNOWLEDGMENTS

Writing a book is a lot like birthing a child. It has a long gestation period during which the author has considerable time to develop ideas about how the book will turn out, which is followed by a mixture of pain and joy during the delivery phase that requires the support of a dedicated team of professionals to assist in translating concepts into reality.

We owe a debt of gratitude to so many colleagues, friends, and family members who supported our dream to create this book. They offered advice, research, insights, sounding boards, professional expertise, and a host of other gifts that have made the journey of creating this work one in which we enjoyed support beyond our expectations. To all of you, we humbly offer our thanks, which is truly insufficient acknowledgment of the impact that your encouragement has had on us.

First to our son, Marc, who is wise beyond his 13 years and whose old soul so patiently waited for the manuscript to be completed, believing all the while that this book would make a positive impact on the world. From your lips to God's ears, Marc!

To our fantastic research team at the University of Michigan, especially Cassie Barnhardt, who was there during the early formulation of the Passion Profiler and spent countless hours researching the literature, helping to develop items, and crunching numbers. You're a lifelong member of the team, Cassie! To Virginia Hamori Ota, also of the University of Michigan, who later stepped in to support refinement of the Passion Profiler, we thank you for your willingness to jump into the deep end of the pool without a flotation device. To Andre Roberson of the Softstage Media Group, we send our gratitude for the many hours of development, testing, and analysis that allowed us to validate the passion archetypes. Your enthusiasm for this project, from concept to fruition, has been encouraging and infectious.

Many friends and colleagues were instrumental in providing early input as concepts in this book were being developed. We especially appreciate the insights of Dr. Kim Sommer, a wonderful Creator/Transformer/Healer, who has been a lifelong friend, a dear sister, and avid supporter of this work; Dr. Sharene Garaman, an Altruist/Healer/ Teacher who so readily contributed to analysis and research that greatly enhanced our understanding of the human psyche; Dr. Dan Ariely for his insight into behavioral economics; Berkley and Heribert von Feilitzsch for the countless dinner discussions and encouragement for this work; Henri Lipmanowitz, the ultimate Conceiver, who pushed the edges of the envelope to challenge our ideas and help us create a better product; Michael R. Gaines and David Gillis, whose Teacher passions taught us about the love of learning; William Pursche, who immediately recognized the value of this work and offered support and encouragement when this book was in its infancy; Dr. Sidney Mazel and Dr. Thierry Poirot, who have shared our corporate journey and helped to validate our experiences; Sumeet Sud, who graciously participated in early testing and insisted on paying for our services—thank you for valuing our work; Rev. Jennings Hobson III, who cautioned us to never forget that this work is in service to others and to connect with the heart—it's a lesson we have always remembered; Sheila Gibbons of Communications Research Associates and playwright Julie Portman for their invaluable assistance in helping us find our voice in the early phases of the project; and Mik Harris, a brilliant Transformer/Discoverer/Builder who enthusiastically read early chapters of this book and offered sage advice on how to structure them. Thanks, Mik, for your willingness to risk painting a mustache on the *Mona Lisa*!

During the completion of this book, an avid fan and family member Charlotte Reid Garrett passed away. We know that she is celebrating the birth of this book along with us. Thank you for a lifetime of loving support.

A host of very gracious clients allowed us to use their organizations as learning laboratories. Sincere thanks to all of you and to all of the clients and leaders around the world who participated in beta testing of the Passion Profiler.

We also appreciate beyond what words can describe the support and encouragement of Dr. Noel Tichy, who has so generously offered his time and insight throughout this project. Noel, you are the epitome of friendship!

Creating a book requires an inspiring environment in which to work. We were fortunate to enjoy the beauty of the North Carolina beach and great food lovingly prepared by our friends there, Rosemarie and Frank Rinaldi. God's country in beautiful Rappahannock County, Virginia, served as home base for the birthing of this book. There is nothing quite like the majesty of the sun rising over the Blue Ridge Mountains to awaken the muse within. We are also grateful to Ralph Wilmot, who so capably and lovingly cared for the farm, the horses, and the dogs, allowing us plenty of unfettered time to write. Deep appreciation is also extended to Cindy and Eddie Wayland, who generously provided another writing retreat in beautiful Chincoteague.

Great work requires a fine literary team. We are blessed to have worked with our wonderful agent, Carol Mann, and a superb and dedicated editor, Mary Glenn, along with the fantastic staff at McGraw-Hill, including Jane Palmieri, editing manager; Cheryl Hudson, senior production supervisor; Marci Nugent, copy editor; Kenya Henderson, marketing manager; Keith Pfeffer, senior director of national accounts group sales; Staci Shands, senior publicist; and their very capable teams. Thank you all for believing in this project!

To the many leaders we interviewed, we extend our sincere appreciation for your candor, honesty, and willingness to reveal your deepest thoughts to readers, believing that they might make a difference in someone else's leadership story. Without you, none of this would have been possible.

Finally, to all of the leaders that we have had as bosses—good and bad, inspirational or cynical—we have learned from you all. Thank you for shaping who we have become and the work we have created.

PASSION PROFILER FREQUENTLY ASKED QUESTIONS

What is the Passion Profiler?

The Passion Profiler is an online assessment tool that measures an individual's purpose as it is expressed externally through observable behaviors manifesting as passions. The instrument identifies and measures ten specific archetypes (or patterns) of passion, and it establishes a hierarchy of the passions that an individual demonstrates. It is grounded in sociocognitive identity development and positive psychology, which is a field of psychology that emphasizes the positive perspectives in an individual's personality and social functioning rather than the deficits and interpersonal pathologies. The intent of those who practice positive psychology is to understand what facilitates individual flourishing.

How has the Passion Profiler been used?

The tool has been applied in a variety of organizational settings. Examples include individual and executive development, team development, succession planning, and strategic organizational development. In addition, it has been utilized with individuals experiencing job and life transitions who are seeking a deeper understanding about what gives meaning to their life in order to determine their future direction. The Passion Profiler also has implications for use within family systems.

Can the Passion Profiler tell me if I am in the right job?

The Passion Profiler report provided with your access code included with this book will provide you with information on the top three archetypes that you carry—what we call your "Passion Archetype Cluster." Details about each of these archetypes can be found in the relevant chapters of this book, which also provide an abbreviated list of potential jobs or functions in which the archetypes will thrive. After logging on to www.thepurposelink.com and clicking on the link to the Passion Profiler tool, complete the Passion Profiler using your access code (found on the reverse side of the back jacket flap). For an additional fee, you may elect to receive the Passion Profiler Comprehensive Analysis. This analysis will provide in-depth information on your top three passions and scoring on all ten passion archetypes, visually represented with graphs and standardized means. It will also provide insights on how your passion archetypes relate to your work. In addition, the extended report will identify how connected you feel to your organization, it will indicate the capacity and propensity you demonstrate for reflecting and making meaning of work and life experiences, and it will highlight the impact your passions have on the Organizational Knowledge Cycle.

What if people who work for me take the Passion Profiler and find that there is limited connection between their passions and their work? Don't I risk losing them?

In our experience, few individuals immediately choose to leave their jobs when they discover a disconnect between their passion archetypes and their jobs. In fact, with the benefit of the Passion Profiler, these individuals are able to more readily identify an outlet for their passions in their current job, thereby strengthening what was once a weak connection. We have observed that employees who are consistently unable to express their passions through their work are much more likely to leave their job or become apathetic and less productive. We believe the Passion Profiler provides a unique mechanism for weaving a connection between one's work and one's passions, thus preventing this attrition or decline of productivity.

What is the Passion Archetype Cluster?

The Passion Archetype Cluster consists of your top three passion archetypes. The cluster represents how you are hardwired from a passion perspective, and it indicates the means by which you are most likely to find fulfillment. The Passion Profiler highlights your top three passion archetypes because individuals are not defined by one passion alone;

we are all a mosaic of our passions. How the three passions in one's cluster operate may vary from person to person. For example, the passions may operate collectively or you may have one passion that is the real driver for the expression of the other two.

Will my passion archetypes always be the same?

It is generally accepted that personality is fluid. However, one's passions tend to be present throughout the life cycle, although they may not be manifested the same over time. For example, the hierarchy of passions in your Passion Archetype Cluster may change over time. What was once the second or third archetype in the cluster may become the first in the cluster depending upon work and life circumstances.

Are there people who don't demonstrate much passion at all?

Yes, but they are in the minority of the population who have completed the Passion Profiler.

How many items will I need to respond to in the Passion Profiler?

There are 158 items plus additional demographic identifiers.

How long will it take me to complete the Passion Profiler?

On average, most respondents are able to complete the tool within 30 to 45 minutes. We suggest that you do not overthink every item but instead, answer as honestly as possible, without worrying about how others would want you to respond. If you are interrupted while completing the Passion Profiler, you may log off and then return to it at another time simply by logging in with your access code and resume answering the next item.

Is it possible to fail the test or look bad?

Absolutely not! There is no pass/fail, and there are no right or wrong answers—only your answers. Remember, this tool is based in positive psychology.

ENDNOTES

Chapter 1

1. Based on working a full 40-hour week from age 21 to retirement at age 65 for an average of 45 weeks per year.

2. Dan Ariely, Uri Gneezy, George Loewenstein, and Nina Mazar, "Large Stakes and Big Mistakes," *Review of Economic Studies*, forthcoming in 2009.

3. Ibid. Also Dan Ariely, Emir Kamenica, and Drazen Prelec, "Man's Search for Meaning: The Case of Legos," *Journal of Economic Behavior & Organization*, vol. 67, 2008, pp. 671–677.

4. Karen M. O'Brien, "Measuring Career Self-Efficacy: Promoting Confidence and Happiness at Work," in Shane J. Lopez and C. R. Snyder, eds., *Positive Psychological Assessment: A Handbook of Models and Measures*, American Psychological Association (APA), Washington, D.C., 2003, chap. 7, pp. 109–129.

5. Ed Diener, *Contributions of the Ed Diener Laboratory to the Scientific Understanding of Well-Being*, Psychology Department, University of Illinois at Urbana-Champaign, www.psych.uiuc.edu/~ediener/Discoveries.htm.

6. Marcela Kogan, "Where Happiness Lies: Social Scientists Reveal Their Research Findings in the Realm of Positive Psychology," *American Psychological Association (APA) Monitor on Psychology*, vol. 32, no. 1, January 2001.

7. Alaina Love, *Expressing Purpose Through Work*, Research Monograph, HRx Renaissance Consortium, Inc., Flint Hill, Va., 2005.

8. Ed Diener and Martin E. P. Seligman, "Beyond Money: Toward an Economy of Well-Being," *Psychological Science in the Public Interest*, vol. 5, no.1, July 2004, pp. 1–31.

9. Ibid.

Chapter 10

1. Robert A. Guth, "Bill Gates Issues Call for Kinder Capitalism," *Wall Street Journal*, January 24, 2008.

Chapter 13

1. International Coach Federation, as reported in Helen Coster, "Baby Please Don't Go," *Forbes*, October 15, 2007.
2. Ibid.
3. Walter Isaacson, *Einstein: His Life and Universe*, Simon & Schuster, New York, 2007.
4. David Whyte, *Crossing the Unknown Sea: Work as a Pilgrimage of Identity*, Riverhead Books, New York, 2001.

Chapter 15

1. *Wall Street Journal*, November 14, 2008, p. 1. (Citibank actually cut 53,000 jobs just following this announcement.)
2. Ibid.
3. *Wall Street Journal*, November 15–16, 2008, p. 1.
4. Ibid.
5. Ibid.
6. Ibid.
7. Ibid.
8. Ibid., p. A8.
9. Kara A. Arnold, Nick Turner, Julian Barling, E. Kevin Kelloway, and Margaret C. McKee, "Transformational Leadership and Psychological Well-Being: The Mediating Role of Meaningful Work," *Journal of Occupational Health Psychology*, vol.12, no. 3, 2007, pp. 193–203.
10. James Collins, *Good to Great: Why Some Companies Make the Leap . . . and Others Don't*, HarperCollins, New York, 2001, pp. 72–73, 89.
11. *The Nestlé Management and Leadership Principles*, courtesy of Nestlé S.A., Vevey, Switzerland.

BIBLIOGRAPHY

Below are the key sources that inspired and informed the writing of this book. We have included works that we hope readers will enjoy exploring and learning from, as much as we have.

Interviews

Ariely, Dan, Ph.D., Duke University. Interview by Alaina Love, September 26, 2008.

Bankston, Karen, senior vice president of the Drake Center, the Health Alliance. Interviews by Alaina Love, April 5, 2007, November 27, 2007, and November 6, 2008.

Barnwell, Ysaye M., Ph.D., Sweet Honey in the Rock. Interview by Alaina Love, August 18, 2007.

Brabeck-Letmathe, Peter, chairman of the board of directors of Nestlé S.A. Interview by Alaina Love, November 26, 2008.

Carson, Benjamin (Ben), M.D., Johns Hopkins Medical Center. Interview by Alaina Love, February 11, 2008.

Eswaran, Vijay, chairman and chief executive officer of the QI Group. Interview by Alaina Love, December 23, 2007.

Fung, Victor K., Ph.D., group chairman of the Li & Fung Group. Interview by Alaina Love, November 20, 2008.

Johns, Chris, editor in chief of the *National Geographic Magazine*. Interview by Alaina Love, August 22, 2008.

Lorange, Peter, Ph.D., IMD. Interviews by Alaina Love and Marc Cugnon, November 3, 2008 and November 10, 2008.

McDonald, Alden J., Jr., president and chief executive officer of Liberty Bank and Trust. Interviews by Alaina Love, April 13, 2007, October 29, 2007, and December 16, 2008.

McWherter, Gregory, Commander, The Blue Angels, U.S. Navy. Interview by Alaina Love, November 25, 2008.

Nelson, Marilyn Carlson, chair and chief executive officer of the Carlson Companies. Interview by Alaina Love, November 27, 2008.

Schoonover, Philip J., former president and chief executive officer of Circuit City. Interviews by Alaina Love, January 3, 2008, September 5, 2008, and October 3, 2008.

Sims, Steve, Ph.D., Whitmire Micro-Gen. Interview by Alaina Love, July 17, 2007.

Vagelos, P. Roy, M.D., former president and chief executive officer of Merck & Co. Interview by Alaina Love and Marc Cugnon, November 13, 2007.

Wood, John, founder and executive chairman of Room to Read. Interview by Alaina Love and Marc Cugnon, December 21, 2007; and interview by Alaina Love, November 21, 2008.

Selected Bibliography

Agbor-Baiyee, W., "Passion for Academic Leadership: An Investigation of the Factors That Motivate and Provide Satisfaction for College and University Presidents," ProQuest Information and Learning, 1996.

Anderson, N., and D. S. Ones, "The Construct Validity of Three Entry Level Personality Inventories Used in the U.K.: Cautionary Findings from a Multiple-Inventory Investigation," *European Journal of Personality*, vol. 17, 2003, pp. S39–S66.

Andrews, Robert, *The Concise Columbia Dictionary of Quotations*, Columbia University Press, New York, 1990.

Ariely, Dan, *Predictably Irrational: The Hidden Forces That Shape Our Decisions*, HarperCollins, New York, 2008.

Ariely, Dan, Uri Gneezy, George Loewenstein, and Nina Mazar, "Large Stakes and Big Mistakes," *Review of Economic Studies*, forthcoming in 2009.

Ariely, Dan, Emir Kamenica, and Drazen Prelec, "Man's Search for Meaning: The Case of Legos," *Journal of Economic Behavior & Organization*, vol. 67, 2008, pp. 671–677.

Arlin, P. K., "Cognitive Development in Adulthood: 5th Stage," *Developmental Psychology*, vol. 11, no. 5, 1975, pp. 602–606.

Arnold, Kara A., Nick Turner, Julian Barling, E. Kevin Kelloway, and Margaret C. McKee, "Transformational Leadership and Psychological Well-Being: The Mediating Role of Meaningful Work," *Journal of Occupational Health Psychology*, vol. 12, no. 3, 2007, pp. 193–203.

Becker, T. E., R. S. Billings, D. M. Eveleth, and N. L. Gilbert, "Foci and Bases of Employee Commitment: Implications for Job Performance," *Academy of Management Journal*, vol. 39, no. 2, 1996, pp. 464–482.

Bennet, A., "Exploring Aspects of Knowledge Management That Contribute to the Passion Expressed by Its Thought Leaders," ProQuest Information and Learning, 2005.

Berg, J. M., J. E. Dutton, and A. Wrzesniewski, "What Is Job Crafting and Why Does It Matter?" Theory to Practice Briefing, University of Michigan Ross School of Business, Center for Positive Organizational Scholarship, August, 2008.

Bierly, P. E., E. H. Kessler, and E. W. Christensen, "Organizational Learning, Knowledge and Wisdom," *Journal of Organizational Change Management*, vol. 13, no. 6, 2000, pp. 595–618.

Borman, W. C., and S. J. Motowidlo, "Task Performance and Contextual Performance: The Meaning for Personnel Selection Research," *Human Performance*, vol. 10, no. 2, 1997, pp. 99–109.

Bossidy, Larry, and Ram Charan, *Execution: The Discipline of Getting Things Done*, Crown Business, New York, 2002.

Boulding, K. E., "General Systems Theory: The Skeleton of Science," *Management Science*, vol. 2, no. 3, 1956, pp. 197–208.

Bronson, Po, *What Should I Do with My Life?* Random House, New York, 2002.

Buckingham, Marcus, and Donald O. Clifton, *Now, Discover Your Strengths,* Free Press, New York, 2001.

Carson, Ben, M.D., with Cecil Murphy, *Gifted Hands: The Ben Carson Story,* Zondervan Books, Grand Rapids, Mich., 1990.

Carson, Ben, M.D., with Gregg Lewis, *Take the Risk: Learning to Identify, Choose and Live with Acceptable Risk,* Zondervan Books, Grand Rapids, Mich., 2008.

Chang, Richard, *The Passion Plan at Work: A Step-by-Step Guide to Building a Passion-Driven Organization,* Jossey-Bass, San Francisco, 2001.

———, "Turning Into Organizational Performance: The Role of Passion in Business Management and Leadership," *Training & Development,* vol. 55, no. 5, May 2001, pp. 104ff.

Chang, Richard, ed., *The Passion Plan: A Step-by-Step Guide to Discovering, Developing, and Living Your Passion,* Jossey-Bass, San Francisco, 2000.

Christiansen, C. H., "Defining Lives: Occupation as Identity: An Essay on Competence, Coherence, and the Creation of Meaning," The 1999 Eleanor Clarke Slagle Lecture, *American Journal of Occupational Therapy,* vol. 53, no. 6, 1999, pp. 547–558.

Collins, Jim, *Good to Great,* HarperCollins, New York, 2001.

Cran, D. J., "Towards Validation of the Service Orientation Construct," *Service Industries Journal,* vol. 14, no. 1, 1994, pp. 34–44.

Czarniawska, B., "Is It Possible to Be a Constructionist Consultant?" *Management Learning,* vol. 32, no. 2, 2001, pp. 253–266.

Debats, D. L., J. Drost, and P. Hansen, "Experiences of Meaning in Life: A Combined Qualitative and Quantitative Approach," *British Journal of Psychology,* vol. 86, 1995, pp. 359–375.

Demerath, L., "Epistemological Identity Theory: Reconceptualizing Commitment as Self-Knowledge," *Sociological Spectrum,* vol. 26, no. 5, 2006, pp. 491–517.

Diener, Ed, *Contributions of the Ed Diener Laboratory to the Scientific Understanding of Well-Being,* Psychology Department, University of Illinois at Urbana-Champaign, www.psych.uiuc.edu/~ediener/Discoveries. htm.

Diener, Ed, and Martin E. P. Seligman, "Beyond Money: Toward an Economy of Well-Being," *Psychological Science in the Public Interest,* vol. 5, no. 1, July 2004, pp. 1–31.

Duchon, D., and D. A. Plowman, "Nurturing the Spirit at Work: Impact on Work Unit Performance," *Leadership Quarterly,* vol. 16, no. 5, 2005, pp. 807–833.

Dutton, J. E., *Energize Your Workplace,* Jossey-Bass, San Francisco, 2003.

Ellemers, N., D. de Gilder, and S. A. Haslam, "Motivating Individuals and Groups at Work: A Social Identity Perspective on Leadership and

Group Performance," *Academy of Management Review,* vol. 29, no. 3, 2004, pp. 459–478.

Ellingson, J. E., P. R. Sackett, and B. S. Connelly, "Personality Assessment Across Selection and Development Contexts: Insights into Response Distortion," *Journal of Applied Psychology,* vol. 92, no. 2, 2007, pp. 386–395.

Frank, Leonard Roy, *Quotationary,* Random House, New York, 2001.

Frankl, Victor E., *Man's Search for Meaning,* Beacon Press, Boston, 2006.

Furnham, A., and R. Drakeley, "Predicting Occupational Personality Test Scores," *Journal of Psychology,* vol. 134, no. 1, 2000, pp. 103–111.

Garreau, Joel, *Radical Evolution: The Promise and Peril of Enhancing Our Minds, Our Bodies—and What It Means to Be Human,* Random House, New York, 2005.

Gladwell, Malcolm, *Blink: The Power of Thinking Without Thinking,* Little, Brown, New York, 2005.

Grant, A. M., "Relational Job Design and the Motivation to Make a Prosocial Difference," *Academy of Management Review,* vol. 32, no. 2, 2007, pp. 393–417.

Hafferty, F. W., "Definitions of Professionalism: A Search for Meaning and Identity," *Clinical Orthopaedics and Related Research,* vol. 449, 2006, pp. 193–204.

Hardy, C., and S. Leiba-O'Sullivan, "The Power behind Empowerment: Implications for Research and Practice," *Human Relations,* vol. 51, no. 4, 1998, pp. 451–483.

Harrison, K., "The Hogan Personality Inventory: A Preliminary Investigation of Its Validity in an Australian Context," *Australian Journal of Psychology,* vol. 55, 2003, pp. 127–127.

Haslam, S. A., C. Powell, and J. C. Turner, "Social Identity, Self-Categorization, and Work Motivation: Rethinking the Contribution of the Group to Positive and Sustainable Organisational Outcomes," *Applied Psychology: An International Review,* vol. 49, no. 3, 2000, pp. 319–339.

Hoffer, Eric, *The Passionate State of Mind, and Other Aphorisms,* Buccanneer Books, Cutchogue, N.Y., 1998. (First edition published in 1955 by Harper & Row.)

Hogan, J., and K. Brinkmeyer, "Bridging the Gap between Overt and Personality-Based Integrity Tests," *Personnel Psychology,* vol. 50, no. 3, 1997, pp. 587–599.

Hogan, J., and R. Hogan, *Motives, Values, Preferences Inventory* (MVPI), Hogan Assessment Systems, Tulsa, Okla., 1987.

Hogan, J., S. L. Rybicki, S. J. Motowidlo, and W. C. Borman, "Relations between Contextual Performance, Personality, and Occupational Advancement," *Human Performance,* vol. 11, no. 2–3, 1998, pp. 189–207.

Isaacson, Walter, *Einstein: His Life and Universe,* Simon & Schuster, New York, 2007.

Jackson, Douglas N., *Leadership Skills Profile* (LSP), Sigma Assessment Systems, Port Huron, Mich., 2003.

Jackson, K. M., and W. M. K. Trochim, "Concept Mapping as an Alternative Approach for the Analysis of Open-Ended Survey Responses," *Organizational Research Methods*, vol. 5, no. 4, 2002, pp. 307–336.

Jha, S. R., "The Tacit-Explicit Connection: Polanyian Integrative Philosophy and a Neo-Polanyian Medical Epistemology," *Theoretical Medicine and Bioethics*, vol. 19, no. 6, 1998, pp. 547–568.

Johnson, J. A., "Predicting Observers' Ratings of the Big Five from the CPI, HPI, and NEO-PI-R: A Comparative Validity Study," *European Journal of Personality*, vol. 14, no. 1, 2000, pp. 1–19.

Jones, Michael, *Artful Leadership: Awakening the Commons of the Imagination*, Pianoscapes, Ontario, 2006.

Kerfoot, K., "On Leadership: Signature Strengths: Achieving Your Destiny," *Nursing Economics*, vol. 23, no. 1, 2005, pp. 46–48.

King, Avrom E., *Choosing to Choose*, Dharma Publishing, Phoenix, 1998.

Kogan, Marcela, "Where Happiness Lies: Social Scientists Reveal Their Research Findings in the Realm of Positive Psychology," *American Psychological Association (APA) Monitor on Psychology*, vol. 32, no. 1, January 2001.

Kutz, M. N., "Passion! Aviation's Best-Kept Leadership Secret a Brief Synopsis of Qualitative Inquiry into One Emotional Aspect of Aviation Leadership," *International Journal of Applied Aviation Studies*, vol. 3, no. 2, 2003, pp. 323–330.

Lall, R., E. K. Holmes, K. R. Brinkmeyer, W. B. Johnson, and B. R. Yatko, "Personality Characteristics of Future Military Leaders," *Military Medicine*, vol. 164, no. 12, 1999, pp. 906–910.

Loo, R., "A Psychometric Evaluation of the General Decision-Making Style Inventory," *Personality and Individual Differences*, vol. 29, no. 5, 2000, pp. 895–905.

Loo, R., and K. Thorpe, "Relationships between Attitudes toward Women's Roles in Society, and Work and Life Values," *Social Science Journal*, vol. 42, no. 3, 2005, pp. 367–374.

Lopez, Shane, and C. R. Snyder, *Positive Psychological Assessment: A Handbook of Models and Measures*, American Psychological Association, Washington, D.C., 2003.

Lorange, Peter, *Thought Leadership Meets Business*, Cambridge University Press, New York, 2008.

Love, Alaina, *Expressing Purpose Through Work*, Research Monograph, HRx Renaissance Consortium, Flint Hill, Va., 2005.

Lucas, J., *The Passionate Organization: Igniting the Fire of Employee Commitment*, AMACOM Books, New York, 1999.

Luther, N., "Integrity Testing and Job Performance within High Performance Work Teams: A Short Note," *Journal of Business and Psychology,* vol. 15, no. 1, 2000, pp. 19–25.

Mabon, H., "Utility Aspects of Personality and Performance," *Human Performance,* vol. 11, no. 2–3, 1998, pp. 289–304.

Markey, P. M., and C. N. Markey, "A Spherical Conceptualization of Personality Traits," *European Journal of Personality,* vol. 20, no. 3, 2006, pp. 169–193.

Marmar, C. R., D. W. Weiss, T. J. Metzler, and K. Delucchi, "Characteristics of Emergency Services Personnel Related to Peritraumatic Dissociation during Critical Incident Exposure," *American Journal of Psychiatry,* vol. 153, no. 7, 1996, pp. 94–102.

Meyer, J. P., T. E. Becker, and R. van Dick, "Social Identities and Commitments at Work: Toward an Integrative Model," *Journal of Organizational Behavior,* vol. 27, no. 5, 2006, pp. 665–683.

Meyer, J. P., T. E. Becker, and C. Vandenberghe, "Employee Commitment and Motivation: A Conceptual Analysis and Integrative Model," *Journal of Applied Psychology,* vol. 89, no. 6, 2004, pp. 991–1007.

Moynihan, D. P., and S. K. Pandey, "The Role of Organizations in Fostering Public Service Motivation," *Public Administration Review,* vol. 67, no. 1, 2007, pp. 40–53.

Nelson, Marilyn Carlson, *How We Lead Matters: Reflections on a Life of Leadership,* McGraw-Hill, New York, 2008.

Odiorne, G. S., "Competence versus Passion," *Training & Development Journal,* vol. 45, no. 5, 1991, pp. 61–64.

O'Kelly, Eugene, *Chasing Daylight: How My Forthcoming Death Transformed My Life,* McGraw-Hill, New York, 2006.

Ones, D. S., and N. Anderson, "Gender and Ethnic Group Differences on Personality Scales in Selection: Some British Data," *Journal of Occupational and Organizational Psychology,* vol. 75, 2002, pp. 255–276.

Parker, N., "Hogan Personality Inventory (HPI)," *Measurement and Evaluation in Counseling and Development,* vol. 21, no. 3, 1988, pp. 139–140.

Pepper, John, *What Really Matters: Service, Leadership, People and Values,* Yale University Press, New Haven, 2007.

Pink, Daniel, *A Whole New Mind: Why Right-Brainers Will Rule the Future,* Riverhead Books, New York, 2006.

Poras, Jerry, Stewart Emery, and Mark Thompson, *Success Built to Last: Creating a Life that Matters,* Plume, New York, 2007.

Schwandt, D. R., "When Managers Become Philosophers: Integrating Learning with Sensemaking," *Academy of Management Learning & Education,* vol. 4, no. 2, 2005, pp. 176–192.

Sheppard, R., K. Han, S. M. Colarelli, G. D. Dai, and D. W. King, "Differential Item Functioning by Sex and Race in the Hogan Personality Inventory," *Assessment,* vol. 13, no. 4, 2006, pp. 442–453.

Sluss, D. M., and B. E. Ashforth, "Relational Identity and Identification: Defining Ourselves through Work Relationships," *Academy of Management Review,* vol. 32, no. 1, 2007, pp. 9–32.

Tett, R. P., J. R. Steele, and R. S. Beauregard, "Broad and Narrow Measures on Both Sides of the Personality–Job Performance Relationship," *Journal of Organizational Behavior,* vol. 24, no. 3, 2003, pp. 335–356.

Tichy, Noel M., and Warren G. Bennis, *Judgment: How Winning Leaders Make Great Calls,* Portfolio, New York, 2007.

Tolle, Eckhart, *A New Earth: Awakening to Your Life's Purpose,* Plume, New York, 2005.

———, *The Power of Now,* Namaste Publishing, Vancouver, 1997.

Trafford, Abigail, *My Time: Making the Most of the Rest of Your Life,* Basic Books, New York, 2004.

Vagelos, P. Roy, and Louis Galambos, *Medicine, Science, and Merck,* Cambridge University Press, New York, 2004.

Weierter, S. J. M., "The Organization of Charisma: Promoting, Creating, and Idealizing Self," *Organization Studies,* vol. 22, no. 1, 2001, pp. 91–115.

Wenger, E. C., and W. M. Snyder, "Communities of Practice: The Organizational Frontier," *Harvard Business Review,* vol. 78, no. 1, 2000, pp. 139ff.

Westenholz, A., "Identity Work and Meaning Arena: Beyond Actor/Structure and Micro/Macro Distinctions in an Empirical Analysis of IT Workers," *American Behavioral Scientist,* vol. 49, no. 7, 2006, pp. 1015–1029.

Wheatley, Margaret J., *Leadership and the New Science,* Berrett-Koehler Publishers, San Francisco, 1994.

Wheatley, Margaret J., and Myron Kellner-Rogers, *A Simpler Way,* Berrett-Koehler Publishers, San Francisco, 1996.

Whyte, David, *Crossing the Unknown Sea: Work as a Pilgrimage of Identity,* Riverhead Books, New York, 2001.

Widiger, T. A., and T. J. Trull, "Assessment of the Five-Factor Model of Personality," *Journal of Personality Assessment,* vol. 68, no. 2, 1997, pp. 228–250.

Wood, John, *Leaving Microsoft to Change the World: An Entrepreneur's Odyssey to Educate the World's Children,* Collins, New York, 2006.

Wrzesniewski, A. C., J. E. Dutton, and G. Debebe, "Interpersonal Sensemaking and the Meaning of Work," *Research in Organizational Behavior,* vol. 25, 2003, pp. 93–135.

Yearout, S., G. Miles, and R. H. Koonce, "Multi-Level Visioning," *Training & Development,* vol. 55, no. 3, 2001, pp. 30ff.

INDEX

ABOUT THE AUTHORS

Alaina Love (Builder/Transformer/Healer) is the president of Purpose Linked Consulting (PLC), a leadership and organizational development consulting firm located in the United States and Thailand. With 26 years of experience, she consults to large multinational Fortune 500 firms as well as small independent companies and hospitals. Since the inception of PLC in 1994, Alaina's work has focused on leadership development, team building, and large-scale organizational change.

Prior to founding PLC, Alaina spent over 12 years with Merck & Co., Inc., a multinational pharmaceutical firm. There, as executive director of human resources, she was responsible for HR services for the sales and marketing division, both domestically and internationally. Her client group included over 15,000 employees worldwide, generating US$12.3 billion in sales. Earlier in her career, Alaina was a research scientist for Merck in the field of immunology, where she worked to develop products for the treatment of diseases such as rheumatoid arthritis and lupus. She later worked in clinical research, with responsibility for monitoring international clinical trials for the antiulcer treatment now known as Pepcid.

In addition to the United States, Alaina has worked with business leaders in Asia, Europe, Canada, and Latin America, and she has lived in Singapore and Thailand. She now lives near Washington, DC, on a horse farm in beautiful Rappahannock County, Virginia.

Marc Cugnon (Transformer/Discoverer/Builder), a native of Belgium, is the CEO and cofounder of Purpose Linked Consulting. With over three decades of business experience, he consults to large multinational firms as well as small independent companies, foreign government organizations, and international universities. His practice at PLC has focused on executive development, cross-cultural team building, strategic business planning, international marketing, and product development.

Prior to founding PLC, Marc enjoyed a 27-year career with three major pharmaceutical companies, focusing on human and animal health products. He has lived and worked in Belgium, the United States, the United Kingdom, France, Hong Kong, Singapore, and Thailand. Marc spent 21 years with Merck & Co., Inc., where he held a number of significant positions, including executive director marketing, Europe, and vice president, Asia-Pacific Region. As VP Asia-Pacific, Marc established eight subsidiaries in the Asian region, including Taiwan, China, Singapore, and Korea. He also served as chairman of the board of Merck-Hangzhou Pharmaceutical Joint Venture.

Marc and his family live in Virginia, where, in his leisure time, he breeds and trains Lusitano horses.

To learn more about the authors and Purpose Linked Consulting, visit www.thepurposelink.com.